Resource
~~Foster~~ Parent's Survival Guide

Learning to care for our most fragile resources .... OUR children!

An Informational Guide
To Caring for At-Risk Children

Resource

~~Foster~~ Parent's Survival Guide

Learning to care for our most fragile resources .... OUR children!

An Informational Guide
To caring for At-Risk Children
In the foster care system

Written by Cheryl Mitchell-Welch, MBA

"Resource Parent Handbook"
Written by Cheryl Mitchell-Welch, MBA

Edited by Martha Penn
Back Cover Photo: Constance Welch

First Printing March 2014

Library of Congress Control Number:		2014903985
ISBN:	Hardcover	978-1-4931-7319-8
	Softcover	978-1-4931-7320-4
	Ebook	978-1-4931-7318-1

This book was printed in the United States of America.

Resource Parent's Handbook can be ordered as follows:

www.cherylmitchellwelch.com
www.finding-solutions.org

Cheryl Mitchell-Welch
731 E. Yosemite Avenue Suite B142
Merced, CA 95340

Rev. date: 04/14/2014

To order additional copies of this book, contact:
Xlibris LLC
1-888-795-4274
www.Xlibris.com
Orders@Xlibris.com
128220

Dedication

September 5, 1989 - December 29, 2011

This book is dedicated to my daughter, Candace Mercedes Welch.
She inspires me to be the best I can be as she showed
the world her best.
She is missed tremendously.

A Parent's Prayer

Now I lay me down to sleep,
I pray my sanity to keep.
For if some peace I do not find,
I'm pretty sure I'll lose my mind.

I pray I find a little quiet,
Far from the daily family riot.
May I lie back and not have to think
About what they're stuffing down the sink,

Or who they're with, or where they're at
And what they're doing to the cat.
I pray for time all to myself
did something just fall off a shelf?

To cuddle in my nice, soft bed
Oh no, another goldfish—dead!
Some silent moments for goodness sake
Did I just hear a window break?

And that I need not cook or clean
well heck, I've got the right to dream
Yes now I lay me down to sleep,
I pray my wits about me keep,
But as I look around I know,
I must have lost them long ago!

~Author Unknown~

Please remember

Everyone has a story.

Your willingness to help children going through a difficult time inspires me to continue my efforts in providing information. The commitment it takes to open your heart, house, and arms to these young people will prove rewarding. Together we can help bring sanity to an insane system.

Don’t Quit

When things go wrong, as they sometimes will,
When the road you’re trudging seems all uphill,
When the funds are low and the debts are high,
And you want to smile, but you have to sigh,
When care is pressing you down a bit.
Rest, if you must, but don’t you quit.

Life is strange with its twists and turns,
As every one of us sometimes learns,
And many a fellow turns about,
When he might have won had he stuck it out;
Don’t give up though the pace seems slow—
You may succeed with another blow.

Often the goal is nearer than,
It seems to a faint and faltering man,
Often the struggler has given up,
When he might have captured the victor’s cup,
And he learned too late when the night slipped down,
How close he was to the golden crown.

Success is failure turned inside out—
The silver tint of the clouds of doubt,
And you never can tell how close you are,
It may be near when it seems so far,
So stick to the fight when you’re hardest hit—
It’s when things seem worst that you must not quit.

—Author unknown

CONTENTS

They sit there waiting, wondering and confused
not sure of their future and left bleeding and bruised.
Sure the wounds will heal and the bruises will go away,
but not until help arrives and love comes their way.
You say you come to help, but sometimes make things worse,
much to your surprise they have built walls
making it difficult to come inside.
They sit there waiting, wondering, and confused,
is there a home they can settle into?
Can they move but only once and find a spot to call their own?
Are the questions on the minds of our youth

—unknown

Special Acknowledgement

My heartfelt thanks goes to the many social workers and advocates who put their heart and soul into improving the lives of children and fighting to create positive change. Your efforts do not go unnoticed.

I want to thank my wonderful family: My son Carl E. Welch Jr., for encouraging me to accept people where they are and help them grow to where they need to be, my daughter, Constance M. Welch, for teaching me to appreciate the gifts in people, my grandsons, Elijah P. Welch and Isaiah M. Welch, for allowing me to join them in laughter and for loving me unconditionally, my mother, Martha Penn, who supports and encourages me to always pursue my dreams, and my dad, James A. Mitchell, who served as a tremendous support to me after the loss of my eldest daughter Candace M. Welch. I love all of you with everything within me. Each of you have played a roll in providing me with inner strength to never give up.

To my friends that supported me through life's most difficult period, thank you for lending a listening ear, a shoulder to cry on, for sending me encouraging words, for liking my photos on Facebook, or simply supporting my ideas. Your friendship means the world to me. A special thank you to Cynthia Bostick, Arrecia Boston, Teresa Campos, Cathy Gilmore, Yolanda Gomez, Yvonne Herrera, Regina Jacobs, Stacy James, Letha Jones, Beatriz Ponce de Leon, Linda Nesbitt, Lisa Ochoa, Lisa Simms, Kristina Stanton, and Anna Yates for your sisterhood. I grew up an only child and God allowed these lovely ladies to enter my life at the right time. I want you to know I love and appreciate you.

I am who I am today due to my many experiences. I want to encourage everyone reading this book to focus on your future and never stop dreaming. You can become who you want to become and do what you want to do.

Stay encouraged!

Purpose of Book

Thinking back more than 10 years ago I was naïve to the child welfare system and unsure of the needs regarding foster children; nor did I realize children in crisis is a growing problem. As a foster parent, I encompassed the enthusiasm, passion, and excitement to perform a job well, however, I lacked the training, skills and knowledge necessary to provide appropriate support to the children in my care. I did the best I could with the skill set I had at that time.

My desire is to take the guess work out of the foster parent experience. I have committed to:

- Equipping foster / resource parents with as much knowledge as they can have to be the best resource for children placed in their care.
- Improving the outcomes for foster youth emancipating from the child welfare system.
- Staying abreast of changes regarding regulations affecting current and emancipated foster youth
- Providing answers to the many questions you may have about being a foster / resource parent
- Increasing your understanding of the Child Welfare System
- Shedding light on the growing problem of children in crisis
- Reducing the number of moves children experience throughout their time in the child welfare system
- Preventing resource parents from making similar mishaps as they embark on their personal journey of helping children
- Encouraging potential resource families to open their homes even if they feel inadequate

Something to remember:

As you read through this book
you will notice foster parent and resource parent
used interchangeably.
The idea of switching from
"foster" to "resource"
allows parents
to adjust their mindset
to thinking of ways or methods
to assist children
placed in their home, instead of
just providing a place
for the children to sleep.

I have included information from the Policies and Procedures Manual, Title 22, Division 6, Chapter 9.5, along with personal knowledge, stories shared by willing participants; however, the names have been changed to maintain confidentiality, in addition to the many other sources identified in the Bibliography.

In The Beginning

1

Overview

The Goal of Child Welfare is:

to ensure children who have been removed
from their biological families
are placed with loving, caring people
who can provide positive experiences
in the midst of their turmoil.

Keeping the goal of Child Welfare in mind as you experience life as a resource parent may be challenging because some decisions made by social workers, lawyers, counselors, judges, and other people involved in the case, may not appear to be in the best interest of the child(ren) placed in your home.

Keep in mind, the Child Welfare personnel may have additional knowledge about the case and is using the knowledge coupled with their experience to determine the best course of action.

You, as the resource parent, are given (need-based) information to assist you in caring for the child(ren) placed in your home. Focus your attention on your part of the equation and provide any important information to your social worker as discovered.

The task of assisting children in crisis is a prodigious undertaking and is needed at an alarming rate as families continue to feel the stress of their circumstances. The challenges may be:

- Incorporating a new member into your family
- Having the knowledge that these children have experienced extreme abuse
- Partnering with people with different goals and beliefs
- Becoming a productive member of a team
- Providing numerous people access to your home
- Ensuring you have time for your own children
- Making everyone's transition a smoothe experience
- Ensuring you have time to invest in another child

Whether you view some or all of these potential challenges as obstacles to overcome or situations you may be unable to handle, the desire of this book is to:

- Increase awareness of the growing problem
- Encourage people to partner with their community to ease the burden of at risk youth
- Assist emancipated foster youth with basic needs

It's time to jump in with both feet and join forces in helping these young people become productive, successful, contributing adults.

History of Foster Care

The history of foster care has evolved over the years and is viewed by some people as an institution that ruins the lives of children; while other people recognize the foster care system as an institution that assist children in becoming more productive citizens. These differing views couldn't be furthest from each other, yet in an effort to provide a detailed comprehensive understanding of the foster care system you are thinking of partnering with or have already partnered with, I have included the history and how the idea came about.

As a researcher, I located thousands of references to foster care that not only provide a detailed description of how foster care came into existence, but also depicts how the system has evolved over the years.

According to the Children's Aid Society website:

> "The idea of foster children started back in the mid 19th Century, when more than 30,000 homeless and neglected children lived on the streets and in the slums of New York City. Charles Loring Brace founded The Children's Aid Society because he believed there was a way to change the future of the orphaned children. Mr. Brace thought removing youngsters from the city streets and placing them with farm families would provide the children an opportunity to escape a lifetime of suffering and develop survival skills."

During the 1850s, Mr. Brace proposed the Orphan Train Movement. The Orphan Train sent children by train to live and work on farms until the early 1900s. Approximately 120,000 children were transported, using the Orphan Train, to new lives. Between 1865 and 1890 orphans transported tripled due largely to the Reconstruction Era, which includes the transformation of Southern states and the abolishment of slavery. Times were turbulent and unstable for many so the belief could be either of the following:

- Parents may have gotten overwhelmed and felt their children needed to learn required skills from an institutionalized environment, or
- Parents may have viewed the Orphan Train as a means to an end. An opportunity for their children to expand their knowledge and increase their prospects, which equals more success

Regardless of the reasons parents placed their children on the Orphan Train, the fact remains there was an increase and no way to predict the outcomes for these children. Now many years later, the concept of foster care has evolved and the outcomes for youth placed in the system have been and continue to be disheartening.

Fast forward to the early 1990s, when Concurrent Planning was birthed. Concurrent Planning is defined as a foster care approach which allows the county to work simultaneously with the birth parents and potential adoptive parents to achieve permanency for children as quickly as possible. Concurrent Planning became the building block for the Adoption and Safe Families Act of 1997, which has two priorities:

- To return children safely to their biological families; however, if that option proves impossible;
- To ensure the foster families are prepared to adopt the children placed in their care.

The main goal is to provide permanency for these children, so they develop a sense of belonging.

The Children's Aid Society is the driving force for a national movement toward community-based foster care.

The community-based foster care model places children in foster homes within their communities to provide continuity with school, friends and other familiar surroundings, thereby reducing the trauma of the placement. This model also allows for the agency to work with birth parents and ensure these families are connected to resources within their neighborhoods.

Taking a leap more than 20 years later, there are now more than 500,000 children within the State of California placed in foster care. Due in part to this increase, there are numerous community-based organizations and governmental agencies working together to improve the Child Welfare System. These improvements include creating efficient child labor laws, adoption and foster care services, public education, regulations, and most recently the Transitional Housing reform.

We will review these improvements in later sections.

Demographics of Foster Youth

According to the most recent statistics gathered from the Adoption and Foster Care Analysis and Reporting System (AFCARS), there are approximately 523,000 children placed in foster care as of 2011. According to some reports this number is decreasing, however, other studies show this number remains stable.

The average length of time a child remains in foster care is approximately 31 months. The average age for a child in the foster care system is 10 years old. Of the thousands of children in the foster care system about 55% are returned to their biological parents. These statistics are alarming!

We've got to do better.

As this book is being written, the number of children in foster care may have changed. Due to this change being unpredictable, the numbers used in the following table was the most current information available at the time of printing.

Once you've reviewed the following table, you should have a clearer picture of the types of placements available to children removed from their biological families and which placement is used more frequently.

Lets review the following table using 523,000 children in placement:

Type of Placements for children in Foster Care in California		
Type of Placement	*Percentage of Children in Placement*	*Number of Children in Placement*
Foster Family Home (Non-Relative)	46%	240,580
Foster Family Home (Relative)	23%	120,290
Institution	10%	52,300
Group Home	9%	47,070
Pre-Adoptive Home	5%	26,150
Trial Home Visit	4%	20,920
Runaway	2%	10,460
Supervised Independent Living	1%	5,230
	100%	523,000

What percentage of children are placed in foster care? ________%

What percentage of children are placed in group homes? ________%

What percentage of children are institutionalized? ________%

How many children are placed with relatives? ________

What percentage of children are placed in Pre-Adoptive homes? ____%

How many children runaway from placements? ________

How many children are placed in institutions? ________

Do you think children placed with relatives have a better outcome than children placed in non-related foster care? ☐ Yes ☐ No

Why or why not? ____

____

This table demonstrates 65% (approximately 339,992) of the children removed from their biological families are placed in non-relative foster care homes, group homes, and institutions. This number equates to over a quarter of a million children needing assistance by loving, warm, sympathetic, and caring people like yourself.

Another alarming fact is the number of children placed in foster care that are placed on psychotropic medications. In Febraury 2012, the television program 20/20 aired a segment titled, "The Wrong Perscription: Foster Youth and Psychotropic Medications."

In this segment the anchor revealed foster youth are five times more likely to be placed on psychotropic medications and nearly 40 percent are taking multiple perscriptions and at a higher dose.

So I ask the question, what are we doing to our future generation?

Some people may answer my question by saying:

- Medicating children is the best action plan to getting their behavior under control
- Medicating children is the worst action plan due to children suffering side effects that could potentially cause irreversable harm in the future

Regardless of your position on perscribing children medication, one cannot argue that often times, youth taking psychotropic medication are not able to understand and comprehend coping skills. These same children may experience a delayed (if ever developed) set of skills to assist them in managing their life after emancipation.

Your role as a resource parent is extremely important!

Are you beginning to see the larger picture?

How can resource parents help?

- Stay aware of the medications the youth placed in your care are perscribed, such as dosage, frequency, etc.
- Research the side effects of each medication, so you can educate your young person on what to expect
- Keep your youth informed when you notice a change in behavior, attitude, etc.
- Ask questions!
- Keep a journal to document your findings
- Keep the social worker informed of changes in behaviors (positive and negative)
- Attend couseling sessions to provide valuable information to the counselor

In short, become an advocate for the child(ren) placed in your home. Speak up when you have concerns, questions or comments. The child's future depends on it!

Demographics of Resource Parents (Foster Parents)

After reviewing a few websites, it has been reported that the typical foster / resource parent is described as:

- A single woman
- Several biological children
- Supported by the welfare or social security disability
- High school dropout whose own children are marginally functioning.
- Inability to help the children with their school work
- Has little hope for a brighter economic or social future.

When I initially read the demographics describing foster / resource parents, I was shocked! Yes there may be some people who fit this description, however, I've been training potential foster / resource parents for the past five years and often times the potential parents are college graduates, married, with at least one person in the home is employed working 40+ hours per week, and is more than capable of assisting children with homework.

The challenge I have with this information is foster / resource parents are being depicted as money hungry, power seeking people who do not have the best interest of the children as a priority. Money can never be the motivator for helping children.

> **I pray my book will equip foster / resource parents with the knowledge needed to improve foster youth outcomes, as well as, provide a more enlighten view on the people who open their homes to assist at risk youth in their care.**

After continued research, I gathered additional information about who foster / resource parents are which includes the ages, marital status, ethnicity, educational level and sex. The results may provide you with a clearer picture.

Age of Foster Parents		**Education**	
18-49	59%	Less than H.S	6%
50-59	30%	High School	56%
60 and over	11%	Associates Degree (2 years)	24%
		Bachelors Degree (4 years)	14%
Marital Status		**Sex**	
Single, Divorced, & Separated	45%	Women	97%
Married	53%	Men	3%
Ethnicity		**Foster Parent Motivations**	
African American	42%	Care and Concern	42%
Hispanic	15%	Financial Gain	29%
White	36%	Combination of Both	29%
Other ethnicities	7%		

After reviewinng the chart above, it may appear that the majority foster / resource parent's are

- Are between 18 and 49 yeas old
- Are married
- Are African American
- Have, at the least, completed high school
- Are females.

**This information is included to show how statistics vary. When articles mention the majority of parents are married, then show the majority of parents are females shows a slight contradiction in information. Be aware of statistics and do not rely solely on the information provided. Complete your own research whenever possible.

Other qualities that potential foster / resource parents should have include:

Compassionate	A feeling of deep sympathy and sorrow for another's misfortune.
Passionate	Expressing and showing strong or intense feelings
Energetic	Possessing an abundance of energy
Courageous	Brave
Empathetic	A sensitivity to one's challenges
Patience	The ability to handle challenging situations without losing one's temper, getting annoyed or irritated
Knowledgable	Well-informed, discerning, and intelligent
Helpful	Giving assistance

You may ask yourself,"Are these qualities all I need to become a professional parent?" The answer is not a simple yes or no. Although the list may make you more successful as a resource parent, you will need to develop your loss manager skills.

The loss manager is one of the most important skills to develop as this skill may assist in reducing the number of blowouts a child experiences throughout their time in placement.

> A blowout is defined as a foster youth moving from one placement to another; often times without the seven (7) day notice.

As a loss manager, you will help foster youth handle various losses they experience after being placed in the foster care system. Some of the losses children experience include:

- The initial placement in the child welfare system
- The loss of their home
- The loss of their parent / guardian
- Moving from one school to another
- Moving from their neighborhood
- Leaving their special toys, clothing, and other personal items at home
- The loss of an animal
- The loss of extended family
- The loss of their siblings (if placed separately)
- The loss of their friends
- The loss of their room
- The loss of their beds
- The loss of familiarity
- The loss of security
- The loss of safety

These losses could have a profound affect on children, so helping them through the loss experience will prove beneficial for the children and yourself.

How are resource parents portrayed in the media?

Often times when resource parents are featured in the media, they are portrayed as greedy, unconcerned, and typically act inappropriate towards the children placed in their care.

Sometimes this portrayal is disturbing and does not depict the true nature of most of the resource parents I have encountered. A few years ago, I saw a movie titled Antwone Fisher starring Derek Luke, a young man growing up in the foster care system. This movie was Denzel Washington's directing debut and was remarkably put together and led me on a terrific journey. While watching the movie, I experienced sadness, anger, and frustration, as I witnessed Antwone deal with rejection, criticism, and sexual abuse.

Antwone grew up angry and withdrawn. Once he turned 18 years old, he enlisted in the military and began to exhibit outbursts. It was recommended he see a Naval psychiatrist. Initially he didn't like the idea of talking to someone about his past, but decided to attend the meetings as he wanted to move forward in his life. As time went on, Antwone developed the strength to deal with the hurts of his past.

Antwone shared his experience prior to foster care and the pain he experienced while in foster care. This poor little guy was molested by the family he lived with; by the family designated to care for him. As Antwone told his story, you could see the pain and anguish in his eyes. I felt horrible for him.

This is an example of how resource parents
are portrayed negatively.

(If you have not yet seen this movie, rent it!)

Stay encouraged! For every bad apple, there are many more good apples. The key is to be one of the good apples, so we can weed out the bad. Together we can increase the number of foster youth who become successful productive citizens.

IMPORTANT TO KEEP IN MIND

Recruiting quality resource parents has proven to be a challenging task, so giving people the good, bad and ugly of the foster care process will hopefully assist people in making the right decisions for their familiy.

The key to becoming a successful parent and partner with the Child Welfare System is to incorporate the following components:

- Attend Support Groups
- Incorporate respite care (Even when the placement is good)
- Attend continuous trainings (Attend as often as possible)
- Establish a good working relationship with the social workers assigned to your case
- Keep the communication lines open
- Keep accurate records

Reason Children Are Removed

There are many reasons children are removed from their biological parent's home. These reasons could include unsafe living conditions, such as a lack of running water or electricity, minimal food, or inadequately supervised on a regular basis, a death of a parent(s), abuse, and neglect.

Once a report is filed with the Child Protective Service, an investigation is completed and if the child(ren) are in imminent danger, they are removed from the home.

The Child Welfare Department has a Factsheet which provides the signs and symptoms of child abuse. The first step in helping abused and neglected children is learning to recognize the signs of abuse and neglect. Although, the presence of one sign does not necessarily mean the child is being abused or neglected. If there are numerous signs, a closer look may be necessary.

- Shows sudden changes in behavior
- Shows sudden changes in school performance
- Has not received help for physical or medical problems identified and brought to the parents attention
- Has learning problems
- Is always watchful, waiting for something bad to happen
- Lacks adult supervision
- Is overly compliant, passive, or withdrawn
- Arrives to school or other activities early, leaves late, and does not want to go home
- The parent ask teachers and or other caregivers to treat the child harshly in regards to discipline
- The child is labeled bad, worthless, burdensome, etc.
- The parents look to the child for care, attention, and to satisfy emotional needs
- The parent never touches the child

The above signs will give you an idea of what to look for when working with children.

Removing children from their homes leads to more damaged and hurting people. The key is to keep the children in their homes with their parents (as long as the situation is safe) and teach the parents or guardians how to care for the children and manage their household.

PREVENTION IS THE KEY TO A SUCCESSFUL COMMUNITY

Types of Abuse

Abuse is the improper treatment which can be viewed as methods to intimidate and or control a person's actions and ability to think and process information on their own. Typically there are four types of abuse associated with children and they include physical abuse, neglect, sexual abuse, and emotional abuse.

Physical Abuse

> can be exhibited through physical acts, such as unexplained burns, bites, bruises, broken bones, black eyes, punching, bullying, hitting a child with an extension cord, or placing a hot iron on a child's back.

Examples of Physical Abuse

A young woman dates a man with six children and is accused of physically and emotionally abusing the eldest daughter while the father is incarcerated on unrelated charges. According to the child, the woman slapped her face, placed a hot iron on her back, and hit her with an extension cord. The child was removed from the home and placed in foster care. The woman was arrested for child abuse.

~~~~~~~~~~~~~~~~~~~~~~

A mother experiencing post-partum throws her four children off the Golden Gate bridge in San Francisco, California.

~~~~~~~~~~~~~~~~~~~~~~

A couple homeschooled their biologial children. The father sexually abused his daughters and fathered several children with them. Once the authorities were notified, the police went to the home to investigate. The man barracated himself and his family in the house. After several hours, the man began shooting various family members, killing all who did not escape. After a long standoff, the father was eventually arrested and charged with several counts of abuse and murder.

~~~~~~~~~~~~~~~~~~~~~~

A mother allowed her boyfriend to discipline (or what the boyfriend considered discipline) her son and the boyfriend beat the child to death.

~~~~~~~~~~~~~~~~~~~~~~

A young mother experiencing mental illness, placed her baby in a microwave for four minutes. She told authorities she thought she placed the baby's bottle in the microwave.

~~~~~~~~~~~~~~~~~~~~~~

Oprah introduced four African American boys adopted from the foster care system at a young age. After the adoption was finalized, the parents decided to homeschool the boys due to educational struggles. Shortly after the boys were removed from the educational system, the parents stopped feeding them regularly and began physically abusing them. By the time these young men were discovered, they were under weight to the point of looking like toodlers. They said they ate anything they could find including paint and wood.

Unfortunately there are more reports of abuse and neglect, but I wanted to include some examples of reported abuse so you will have an idea of what is happening in the communities in which you live. You, as a foster / resource parent, are a mandated reporter. You will be required to report abuse of a child of any form. (See the Mandated Reporter section)
~~~~~~~~~~~~~~~~~~~~~~

Neglect

may be identified by a child's frequent absence from school, begging or stealing food or money, lacks medical, dental or vision care, is consistently dirty or smells, lacks sufficient clothing for the changes in weather, and or the child states no one is home to care for them.

Sexual Abuse

may be identified by a child having difficulty walking or sitting, bedwetting, experiences a sudden change in appetite, demonstrates bizarre, sophisticated or unusual sexual knowledge or behavior, runs away, becomes pregnant or contracts a venereal disease.

Emotional Maltreatment / Abuse

may be identified by a child's extreme behaviors, such as overly compliant, demanding, or aggression, name calling, yelling, degrading, humiliating or emotional oppression.

Substance Abuse

can be defined as a pattern of harmful use of any substance for mood-altering purposes. These substances may include inhalants, solvents, meth and anabolic steroids. When caregivers experience substance abuse, they may not think as clear, so their decisions may be faulty.

**Special Note: If a child is exhibiting the above behaviors, more information is needed to determine if the child is experiencing some type of abuse or neglect. REPORT IT!

Placement Options

Foster Family Homes

Foster Family Homes are defined as private homes licensed by the state, where foster children are given care and supervision 24 hours a day. These placements are the least restrictive and most favorable environment for children involved in the child welfare system due to no fault of their own.

Group Homes

Group Homes are defined as licensed facilities that provide 24-hour non-medical care and supervision to children in a structured environment. Group homes are considered the most restrictive out-of-home placement for children involved in the child welfare system.

Residential Treatment Centers

Residential Treatment Centers provide services to children suffering from mental illness or emotional disorder. These facilities are staffed with qualified professionals 24 hours a day, 7 days a week. These facilities have been established for children who are unable to function in a family setting without endangering themselves or someone else.

Information You Need to Know to Become a Resource Parent

2

Confidentiality

Confidentiality is not only expected, but required when dealing with sensitive subjects such as foster children who have been abused or neglected. If you read something or are informed of the child's history you are to hold the information in strict confidence. For example:

> When you enroll the child in school, the only information the school needs is information related to the child's education. i.e. Individual Education Plans (IEP), last school attended, any known disabilities, etc. Telling the school why the child entered foster care is not appropriate and should not be discussed. If you discuss the child's history with anyone other than the social worker and or counselor, you could be in violation of the child's right to privacy.

IMPORTANT: All too often parents want to share stories of their children with family and friends, but please **DO NOT** share your foster child's information. If the foster child wants to share his/her story, they can and you can use this opportunity to gain a better understanding. You, as resource parents, are not afforded this opportunity. Be respectful!

Sometimes children, who become aware of private information, may make comments that prove embarrassing. Therefore you want to keep information shared with your children to a minimum.

The Selection Process: A Step-by-Step Guide for Becoming A Resource Parent

Becoming a resource parent could prove overwhelming. Listed below are the steps you may need to follow. Of course the process may vary in order, but could take approximately three to four months to complete.

- Call the County Licensing office or the Foster Family Agency Schedule Orientation

- Attend Orientation or Informational Meeting
  - To obtain basic information about foster care

- Sign up for Training (Typically 27-hour Foster / Adopt Pride)
  - Learn how to handle various situations and gain an understanding of what foster children experience.

- Complete an application
  - Introduce yourself and your family, provide history about your past relationships, discuss why you want to be a resource parent, provide references, educational background, criminal history, and discuss how you resolve differences, etc.

- Complete an At-Home consultation
  - Your house is inspected to ensure you have the right number of bed space, storage space, and to ensure your house is safe with no major discrepancies.

- Fingerprint
  - Child Abuse Index
  - Department of Justice (DOJ)
  - Federal Bureau of Investigation (FBI)

- Tuberculosis (TB) Test

- Receive certification & a child is placed in your home

Juvenile Dependency Process Example

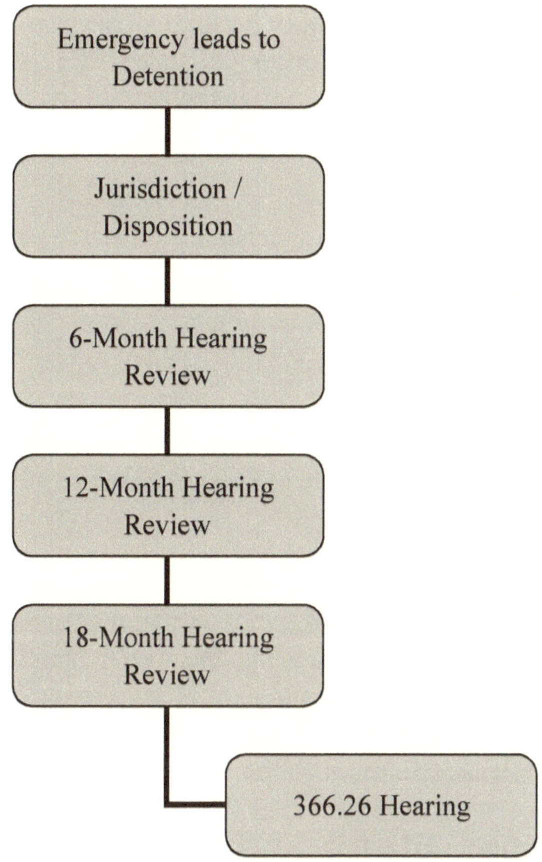

The above picture depicts the step-by-step process a child experiences once removed from their home.

This system is complicated and is included to give you a brief overview of how the system works. For details of your foster child's case, see the assigned social worker.

The goal of the dependency court is to ensure the child's safety. The reason the court gets involved is due to specific circumstances that caused the child to be in imminent danger. If the child is perceived to be in imminent danger, the child will be removed from the home and placed in the child welfare system i.e. foster care.

Initially, a call is placed to Child Protective Service (CPS) and an Emergency Response Social Worker will take the report. The social worker will determine through an investigation if the child is in imminent danger and take appropriate actions for the child to be removed from the home.

For the sake of the example,
let us imagine that the person making the report states
the child is in imminent danger.

The next step, a social worker will go out to the location of the reported abuse and perform an investigation. The child is removed from the home, placed in foster care, a case is opened and the following court actions are taken:

- **Detention Hearing** (W/I Section 319, Rules of the Court 5.674)—which is where the government has to provide evidence to the judge proving the minor should be detained. During this hearing the judge will determine if the evidence presented is enough to detain the minor and if not enough to detain, release the minor to the parents.

- **Jurisdiction Hearing** (W/I Section 300, 350, 355.1, California Rules of the Court 5.682, 5.684, 5.686, 5.688)—the government has to prove that the injuries to the minor was unexplained, non-accidental, and were caused by abuse or neglect.

- **Disposition Hearing** **May be combined with Jurisdiction Hearing**(W/I Section 360-362.6, California Rules of Court 5.686, 5.690, 5.695, 5.700, 5.705)—the government has to provide clear and convincing evidence of substantial risk of danger to the child.

- **6-Month Review Hearing** (W/I Section 364, 366.21, 366.22, California Rules of the Court 5.706, 5.708, 5.710)—the minor shall be returned to the parents unless there is a substantial risk to the minor's physical or emotional well-being, or when the parents have failed to participate regularly in any court-ordered treatment program.

- **12-Month Hearing** (W/I Section 366.21.f, 364, California Rules of the Court 5.715)—the minor shall be returned to the parents unless there is a substantial risk to the minor's physical or emotional well-being, or when the parents have failed to participate regularly in any court-ordered treatment program. **When the minor is not returned to the parents, it is presumed services will be terminated unless there is a substantial probability the minor will be returned to the custody of the parents within 6 months, or unless reasonable services have not been provided to the parents.

- **18-Month Hearing** (W/I Section 366.22, California Rules of Court 5.720)—the minor shall be returned to the parents unless there is a substantial risk to the minor's physical or emotional well-being, or when the parents have failed to participate regularly in any court-ordered treatment program.

    - Selection and Implementing Hearing (Permanency Planning) (W/I Section 366.26, California Rules of Court 5.705, 5.725)—120 days from order terminating reunification services. Options:

        - Long Term Foster Care
        - Guardianship
        - Adoption Planning

    - Post Permanency Planning (PP) Hearing

Important Regulations

According to the Child Welfare Information website, a number of Federal laws provide standards and guidance for State foster care adoption programs. The primary responsibility for child welfare services rests with the States, and each State has its own legal and administrative structures and programs that address the needs of children and families. However, States must comply with specific Federal requirements and guidelines in order to be eligible for Federal funding under certain programs.

We will highlight a few regulations; however, we encourage you to perform research to become more familiar with the regulations that affect you as a resource parent. The following regulations include:

Child Abuse Prevention and Treatment Act (CAPTA) of 1974

Indian Child Welfare Act (ICWA) of 1978

Adoption Assistance and Child Welfare Act of 1980

Child Abuse Prevention, Adoption, and Family Services Act (CAPAFS) of 1988

Adoption and Safe Families Act of 1997

Child Abuse Prevention and Enforcement Act of 2000

Keep Children and Families Safe Act of 2003

Safe and Timely Interstate Placement of Foster Children Act of 2006

Fostering Connections to Success and Increasing Adoptions Act of 2008

Assembly Bill 12 (AB12)

Child Abuse Prevention and Treatment Act (CAPTA) of 1974

The Child Abuse Prevention and Treatment Act (CAPTA) of 1974 regulation dated January 31, 1974 provided financial assistance for the prevention, identification, and treatment of child abuse and neglect.

Indian Child Welfare Act (ICWA) of 1978

The Indian Child Welfare Act (ICWA) of 1978 was formed to establish standards for the placement of Indian children in foster and adoptive homes and to prevent the breakup of Indian families. ICWA, is a federal law that was passed in response to the alarmingly high number of Indian children being separated from their families by both public and private agencies. The intent of congress under ICWA was to protect the best interests of Indian children and to promote the stability and security of Indian tribes and families.

When ICWA applies to a child's case, the child's tribe and family will have an opportunity to be involved in decisions affecting services for the child. A tribe or parent can also petition to transfer jurisdiction of the case to their own tribal court.

> This regulation caused a stir in a training because the participants could not understand why this population established a law to protect their children and other ethnicities do not have a similar law on the books.

Adoption Assistance and Child Welfare Act of 1980

The Adoption Assistance and Child Welfare Act of 1980 provides a monetary assistance program for children being adopted. This act improved the child welfare, social services, and aid to families with dependent children programs by dramatically decreasing the number of children left in foster care.

The Adoption Assistance and Child Welfare Act major provisions include:

- Required the States to make adoption assistance payments, which takes into account the circumstances of the adopting parents and the child;
- Defined a child with special needs as a child who:
    - Cannot return to the parent's home
    - Has a special condition such that the child cannot be placed without providing assistance
    - Has not been able to be placed without assistance
- Required the State, as a condition of receiving Federal foster care matching funds, make "reasonable efforts" to prevent removal of the child from the home and or return a child to their home as soon as possible
- Required participating States to establish reunification and preventive programs for all children in foster care
- Required the State to place a child in the least restrictive setting and possibly a home close to the parent's home
- Required the court or agency to review the status of a child in any nonpermanent setting every 6 months to determine what is in the best interest of the child, with emphasis on returning the child home as soon as possible
- Required the court or administrative body to determine the child's long term options, which may include returning to parents, adoption, or continued foster care, within 18 months after initial placement into foster care

The induction of this Act marked the turning point for improving outcomes for children placed in the foster care system.

Child Abuse Prevention, Adoption, and Family Services Act (CAPAFS) of 1988

Established to amend the Child Abuse Prevention and Treatment Act (CAPTA) and broadened the scope of research to include investigate and judicial procedures applicable to child abuse cases and the national incidence of child abuse and neglect. This Act also expanded the Adoption Opportunities program to increase the number of minority children placed in adoptive families, with an emphasis on recruitment of and placement with minority families; to provide for post-legal adoption services for families who have adopted special needs children, and to increase the placement of foster care children legally free for adoption.

Adoption and Safe Families Act of 1997

The Adoption and Safe Families Act of 1997 was signed into law to improve the safety of children, promote adoption and other permanent homes for children and to support families.

Child Abuse Prevention and Enforcement Act of 2000

This Act was established to address concerns about the level and quality of responses to reports of child maltreatment. Also, the Act authorized the use of Federal law enforcement funds by States to improve the criminal justice system in order to provide timely, accurate, and complete criminal history record information to child welfare agencies, organizations, and programs that are engaged in the assessment of activities related to the protection of children, including protection against child sexual abuse, and placement of children in foster care.

Keep Children and Families Safe Act of 2003

The Keeping Children and Families Safe Act of 2003 reauthorizes the Child Abuse Prevention and Treatment Act (CAPTA), which helps states improve practices in preventing and treating child abuse and neglect, includes a basic state grant program for improving the child protective services (CPS) system infrastructure, as discretionary grant program for research, program demonstrations, training, and other innovative activities, and a grant program focused on community-based prevention efforts.

Safe and Timely Interstate Placement of Foster Children Act of 2006

The Safe and Timely Interstate Placement of Foster Children Act of 2006 was designed to improve protections for children and to hold States accountable for the safe and timely placement of children across State lines.

Fostering Connections to Success and Increasing Adoptions Act of 2008

The Fostering Connections to Success and Increasing Adoptions Act was signed into law by President Bush in 2008 and states this act will help hundreds of thousands of children and youth in foster care by promoting permanent families for them through relative guardianship and adoption and improving education and health care.

Assembly Bill 12 (AB 12)

Assembly Bill 12 was signed into law on September 30, 2010. This bill, which becomes effective on January 1, 2012, implements provisions of the Federal Fostering Connections to Success and Increasing Adoptions Act of 2008 (PL 110-351) in California.

One of the provisions of the Federal bill allows states to extend foster care up to age 21 to young adults who meet the federal participation criteria after age 18. California has opt to initiate the age limit by steps, i.e. by age 19 in 2012; by age 20 in 2013; and may go up to age 21 depending on additional money being appropriated by the Legislature in 2014.

A new foster care placement option called THP-PLUS-FC was created via AB 12 as a placement option for these young adults called Non-Minor Dependents (NMDs).

This law is the first of many to follow that has innovatively targeted the emancipated foster youth in an effort to improve outcomes.

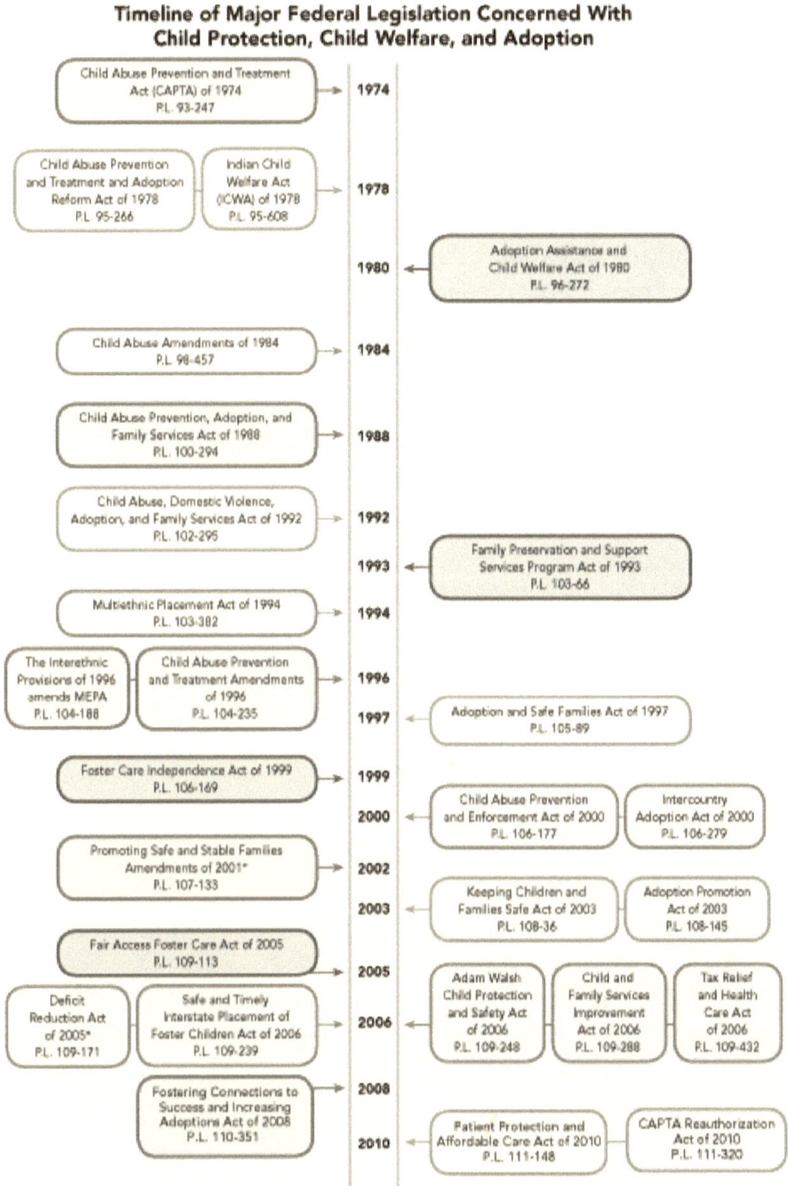

*Some acts were enacted the year following their introduction in Congress.

Community Licensing

According to the California Department of Social Services (CDSS) website, "The mission of community licensing is to promote the health, safety, and quality of life of each person in community care through the administration of an effective collaborative regulatory enforcement system." This mission is accomplished by:

- Promoting startegies to increase voluntary compliance
- Providing technical assistance to and consulting with care providers
- Working collaboratively with clients, their families, advocates, care providers, placement and regulatory agencies, and other related programs
- Training staff in all aspects of the licensing process
- Educating the public about the Community Care Licensing Division (CCLD) and community care options
- Promoting continuous improvement and efficiency throughout the community care licensing system

Department of Social Services
Community Care Licensing Division
Statewide Children's Residential Program
744 P Street, MS 8-3-54
Sacramento, CA 95814

(916) 651-5380—Ofc
(916) 657-1657—Fax

Website: http://www.ccld.ca.gov/res/pdf/childres_rolist.pdf

The Child Care Licensing Program licenses and monitors Family Child Care Homes and Child Care Centers in an effort to ensure that they provide a safe and healthy environment for children who are in care.

Using the above information, call the office or log onto the website to obtain the nearest office to your location.

Making an Informed Decision

3

County vs. Foster Family Agencies (FFA)

County	Foster Family Agencies (FFA)
• Receive children from within County	• Receive children from within the state
• Certifies your home for foster children	• License your home for foster children
• Required to make monthly visits	• Requires to make weekly visits
• May provide less services	• May provide more services
• Social Workers may be more difficult to get in touch with	• Social Workers may be easier to reach
• Social Workers write reports directly to judge	• Social Workers write reports to the County, which may be included in report to judge
• Reimbursement may be lower	• Reimbursement may be higher

I want to caution you—some foster family agencies say they provide additional services. Hold these agencies accountable. Be sure your agency offers all of the services they advertise.

Your goal is to help children; not just house them!

Searching for the right Foster Family Agency (FFA)

Choosing the right Foster Family Agency will be key to a rewarding experience as a resource parent. There are many agencies to partner with. The differences between these agencies may vary from county to county depending on what the needs are in the varying areas.

Follow the listed steps to ensure your homework is complete prior to making your decision:

Research to develop a list of local foster family agencies in your area.

- Complete an internet search, using Google or Yahoo
- If you have access to the Yellow Pages of the phone book, look in the Foster Care Agencies section
- Contact your Social Service Agency and ask them for a list of agencies they place their children with (see County Contact section of this book)

Keep detailed notes when calling the variest agencies; notice the friendlinest of the person answering the phone

Ask questions. Listed below are a few questions you may want to ask:

- What is the process of becoming a resource parent with your agency?
- How often are orientations held, when is the next orientation?
- What are the ages of the children placed through your agency?
- Do I have a choice in the child I want in my home?
- Are there any fees associated with the services? If so, how much?
    - Fingerprinting?
    - Background?
    - Orientation?
    - Pre-Training?
    - Post-Training?
- How often does a social worker come to my house?

- What are the expectations for resource parents?
- How many children can be placed in my home at one time?
- Has the agency worked with families like mine?
- Will they work with children in other counties / states?
- How much of the child's background will I be given?
- When will the children arrive to my home?
- If there is a problem with a child placed in my home, what is the procedure for dealing with this problem?
- Is there assistance in providing transportation to appointments? (i.e. doctors, family visits, court, recreational, etc.)
- What type of support is provided for resource parents?
- How often are trainings for resource parents?
- What are the various training topics?
- Can you attend the resource parent support group prior to signing with your agency?
- What type of support is provided to foster youth?
- Does the agency support adoption efforts?
- Does the agency offer support groups, individual consultation or theraphy after the adoption is final?

After calling the variest agencies to ask the questions on the previous page, what did you think of their responses. Ask yourself the following questions:

- Was the person you spoke with professional? Knowledgable? Respectful?
- Did the person make you feel comfortable?
- Did you feel the person was annoyed with your questions?
- Were your questions answered respectfully?
- Was the information clear, realistic, and detailed?
- Did the person encourage your questions?
- Did the person speak about the children and birth families respectfully?
- Was the Adoption process explained clearly?
- Were you encouraged to follow up via phone or email for additional information?
- Did the person downplay the difficulties of working with at risk children?

- Did the person over-emphasize the negativity of working with at risk children?
- Are there any issues you have identified?

Look for a balance of realism and enthusiasm!

Now you have the answers to your questions . . . . make your choice. Determine from your answers which agency best "fits" your family and lifestyle? If at all possible, speak to current parents partnering with the agency. Keep in mind, no agency is perfect, no prospective parent is perfect. Expecting a few bumps along the road will reduce your frustration.

Teamwork

> It is amazing how much you can accomplish when it doesn't matter who gets the credit.
>
> —unknown

A team is described as more than one person with different responsibilities. Teamwork is action performed by the team towards a common goal. Using this definition, the foster care program has many members on the team and all members perform varying duties to ensure the children in care are receiving the best possible solutions for their challenges.

For example, during the resource parent pre-training classes, there is a section discussed regarding teamwork. During this class, team members are identified and they include:

- Foster Child
- Resource Parent
- Biological Parents
- Grandparents
- Extended Family Members (aunts, uncles, cousins, etc.)
- Counselors
- County Social Workers / FFA Social Workers

- Teachers
- Trainers
- Coaches
- Pastors / Ministers
- Foster Care School Liaison
- Neighbors
- School Administrators
- Store Clerks
- Church Congregation
- Others ______________________________
- And anyone who is involved with your foster child before, during and after the foster care experience

Questions to ask the Social Worker before a child is placed in your home

1. Is this placement a long-term or short-term placement?
2. Is the child male or female?
3. What age is the child?
4. What grade is the child?
5. What is the name of the last school the child was attending?
6. Are there any special medical, physical or emotional conditions?
7. Are there any developmental issues?
8. What type of abuse has the child experienced?
9. How soon is placement?
10. Will I need a car seat?
11. Do I need to pick the child up? OR Are you going to drop him/her off?
12. Does the child have any medical, counseling or other appointments already scheduled? If so, where?
13. Does the child have a Medi-Cal card?
14. Has this child been in foster care before?
15. Is the child moving from a foster home to mine? If so, why are they moving?
16. Does the child have allergies?
17. Does the child have asthma? Inhaler?
18. Is the baby breastfeeding?
19. Does the child have siblings?
20. What is this child's current status in the Child Welfare process?
21. Does the child have an Individual Education Plan (IEP)?
22. Does the child have a religious affiliation?
23. How often, if any, are family visits?

Again, if you can think of other questions to ask the social worker prior to the child being placed in your home, write the questions here:

1. ______________________________
2. ______________________________
3. ______________________________

**If you think of additional questions, please submit these questions to my website. I would love to include them in the future.

The Facts about Maltreatment in Foster Care

Allegations of children being abused in foster care have been reported for many years, although the subject is not a matter of discussion regularly. I want to include this section in the book to make you aware of incidents that have happened and how it is important in your role as resource parent to be extra careful while caring for children who are involved in the child welfare system.

> I do want to add that although abuse does happen to children in care, the percentage has been reported as less than 2%. When incidents are reported the allegations are investigated. If the person or people are found guilty, they will be prosecuted to the extent the law allows.

Listed below are a few incidents that have come to light:

According to the National Youth Law website:

> On May 13, 2005, a 14-month old foster child was found dead after being left alone with other young children. The Clark County coroner's office stated the child was scaled to death and determined the boy's death was a homicide. The foster parent Sally Jones-Johnson faces six felony charges of child neglect because police alledge she neglected the six foster children, ages 7 months to 6 years, living at her North Las Vegas home.

Carla Crowder from the Denver Rocky Mountain News reported

> A 2 ½ year old toddler who was placed in foster care was beaten to death for soiling his pants after the foster father had been drinking at a party.

In California:

> A foster mother arrived home after grocery shopping and started unpacking her vehicle. She removed her four year

> old foster son from his carseat and proceeded to remove the groceries. She was consumed with removing the groceries from the vehicle and failed to keep a watchful eye the toddler. After she unloaded the groceries from the vehicle, she noticed the young boy was not around. She searched the house for him, calling his name and the boy did not respond. Finally after several minutes of searching, she found the young lifeless body of the four year old toddler face down in the swimming pool in the backyard.

According to the Merced Sun Star:

> On August 21, 2009, a 51-year old Los Banos woman was convicted of abusing her 16 year old foster daughter. It was reported the woman hit the girl with tree branches on her legs and face, cut her with a knife, threaten to cut off her fingers and bit her several times. This woman was sentenced to jail for the abuse reported by the girl and a neighbor.

These stories are alarming!
Although the percentage of abused children in care is less than 2%, any number of children facing additional abuse is horrific and cannot be tolerated.

Resource Parent Frequently Asked Questions

1. Who are the children?

The children in the California's foster care system vary in age from newborn to 18 years old and also vary in ethnicity. The ethnic groups represented in the child welfare system include American Indian (Alaskan Native), Asian, African American, Hispanic, White (Non-Hispanic). Neglect, abuse, and maltreatment does not discriminate amongst ethnic groups or socio-economic levels.

However, studies have indicated there are an overrepresentation of America Indian and African American children in the child welfare system. According to the U.S. Census Bureau's 2008 American Community Survey, the following is true:

Race/Ethnicity	Percentage of Total Child Population	Percentage of Children in Foster Care
American Indian / Alaskan Native	1%	2%
Asian	4%	1%
African American	14%	31%
Hispanic	22%	20%
White, Non-Hispanic	56%	40%

The chart on the previous page illustrates African American children are only 14% of California's population, but are 31% of the population in the child welfare system. This information is distressing and should cause alarms to go off within the African American community. If this trend continues, the African American population will not only suffer, but will continue to experience a disconnect within their communities.

2. What is the role of a resource parent?

Resource parents have many responsibilities to their families, the child placed in their home, the agency in which they partner, and to the rest of the child welfare team. The goal of the resource parent is to provide a supportive and stable environment, which includes nurturing and disciplining the children placed in their home. Some of the roles you will operate in as a resource parent include a behavioral management specialist, an advocate, a teacher, and a caregiver. The resource parents partner with social service personnel to reunite children with their biological parents whenever possible.

3. How do I become a resource parent?

If you are seeking to become a resource parent through the foster family agency, you will need to be licensed to operate a resource home or certified through the county. The process requires attending the initial informational session, then turning in the necessary paperwork and adhering to a background check. Once the paperwork has been completed, a social worker will come to your home and meet you family and check your home for the minimal space requirements to determine the type of child best suited for your home. (i.e. age, health, issues, and gender)

4. Can I afford to be a resource parent?

Resource parents must have their own financial means to manage their personal expenses prior to having a child placed in their home. However, you will receive a monthly reimbursement to assist you in caring for the children placed in your care. The reimbursement should

be used to cover living expenses, clothing, school, and extra-curricular activities, along with anything else the child needs throughout the month.

5. **What if my foster child gets sick?**

If your foster child gets sick, it is your responsibility to provide the necessary supervision for your child. Do not contact the social worker to assist with supervision. You will need to contact the social worker if the child is hospitalized and or major decisions need to be made regarding the care of the child. The medical expenses will be covered by the Medi-Cal program and you should receive a Medi-Cal card for each child placed in your home.

**If you do not have a Medi-Cal card for each child placed in your home, contact the social worker to obtain a temporary card until the permanent card can be ordered.

6. **Can I still work outside of the home, once a foster child is placed in my home?**

Yes you can work and working is recommended as you will need to have your own resources to manage your current household expenses. For the parents who are working outside of the home, you will be required to provide appropriate child care arrangements. The payments for the child care service should be taken from your monthly reimbursement.

**There may be times when you can qualify for government child care programs to cover the expenses; however, this is not always possible.

7. **Are there age limits / requirements in becoming a resource parent?**

There are no age requirements to becoming a resource parent, however, you must be in good health, have plenty of energy to keep up with the children, and be willing to work as a team to assist the children in your care. Retired resource parents make excellence team members as their time may be more flexible.

Special Note:

> County placing agencies have indicated a particular need for resource homes that are willing to provide care to adolescents, sibling sets, and emergency placements.

For additional information:

Call toll-free at 1-00-KIDS-4-US (1-800-543-7487) or write to:

Recruitment Network Development Unit
Child & Youth Permanency Branch
California Department of Social Services
744 P Street—M/S 14-78
Sacramento, CA 95814

Thought Provoking Questions

Take a few minutes to reflect on the following questions. Answer these questions openly and honestly:

Yes	No	
☐	☐	Is becoming a resource parent the right decision for me?
☐	☐	Do I have the qualities and characteristics to be a successful resource parent?
☐	☐	Am I deciding to become a resource parent for the right reason?
☐	☐	Do I have any unresolved personal trauma, loss or grief issues that may prevent me from recognizing and or meeting the needs of the foster youth placed in my care?
☐	☐	Is my entire household ready for the changes of adding an additional person to the household?
☐	☐	Do I have the support of my extended family?
☐	☐	Am I ready?

Meeting the Needs of Our Children

4

Meeting the Needs of Our Children

It is important to meet the developmental needs of children who have experienced trauma. Listed below are some of the steps that may assist children move beyond their traumatizing experience:

1. Ask questions and listen to the answer
2. Determine the problem
3. Acknowledge the child's feelings about the problem
4. Decide the best course of acion in dealing with the problem
5. Stay focused
6. Develop a team of professionals
7. Revisit as often as necessary

It is understood often times adults fail to recognize the magnitude of the amount of stress children experience.

1. **Ask questions and listen to the answer**

   Sit down with your young person and ask open-ended questions to get a dialogue started. Be sure to listen openly with no judgment.

2. **Determine the problem**

3. **Acknowledge the child's feelings about the problem**

   When a child is placed in your home, you may not have all of the information regarding his / her abuse. The key is to acknowledge the child's feelings about the problem providing the means of validating and confirming, then letting them know it is okay that they feel the way they feel.

4. **Decide the best course of action in dealing with the problem**

   Keeping developmental stages in mind. This is an important part of the equation as without this piece, you may have inappropriate reactions or responses to the children which could prove more detrimental then advantageous.

5. **Stay focused**

   Keep your focus on the child's challenges in an effort to be available for them during a crisis

6. **Develop a team of professionals**

   Use the school as a resource. Schools can provide children with routines, structure, and a sense of normalcy. If a child remains at the same school, keep same connections, and participate in the same activities—the child's transitions will be smoother. Not to mention the school personnel may already be familiar with the child and could serve as a tremendous resource for you.

7. **Revisit as often as necessary**

   Even though the child may have shared their experiences, always be prepared to listen again as the story may reveal additional information that they may feel comfortable sharing after more time has elasped.

List of Challenges

Listed below are some of the challenges some of the children experience. I encourage you to perform your own research regarding the topics below. Researching these topics will allow you to be:

- More equip to handle the challenges
- An active member on the team
- Able to assist your child deal with difficult situations

Abandonment
Addictions (Alcoholism, shopping, etc.)
Attention Deficit Hyperactivity Disorder (ADHD)
Anger and Aggression
Anxiety and Worry
Attachment
Complusive Eating and Not-Eating
Conduct Disorder
Depression
Drug Use
Food Allergies
Loss
Low Self-Confidence
Low Self-Esteem
Low Self-Worth
Obsessive Compulsive Disorder
Oppositional Defiance Disorder
Procrastination
Rage
Relationship Problems
Sleep Problems
Smoking
Speech Problems

Of course there are additional challenges these young people could experience, the list above will provide you with a starting point.

PERSONAL RIGHTS
Children's Residential Facilities

YOU HAVE THE RIGHT:

- To live in a safe, healthy, and comfortable home and to be treated with respect.
- To be free from physical, sexual, emotional, or other abuse, or corporal punishment.
- To be free from discrimination, intimidation, or harassment based on sex, race, color, religion, ancestry, national origin, disability, medical condiction, or sexual orientation or perception of having one or more of those characteristics.
- To receive adequate and healthy food and adequate clothing.
- To wear your own clothing.
- To possess and use personal possessions, including toliet articles.
- To receive medical, dental, vision, and mental health services.
- To be free of the administration of medication or chemical substances, unless authorized by a physician.
- To contact family members (unless prohibited by court order) and social workers, attorneys, foster youth advocates and supporters, Court Appointed Special Advocates (CASA) and probation officers.
- To visit and contact brothers and sisters, unless prohibited by court order.
- To contact Community Care Licensing Division of the State Department of Social Services or the State Foster Care Ombudsperson regarding violations of rights, to speak to representatives of these offices confidentially and to be free from threats or punishments for making complaints.
- To be informed by the caregiver of the provisions of the law regarding complaints.
- To make and receive confidential phone calls and send and receive unopened mail (unless prohibited by court order).
- To attend religious services and activities of your choice.
- To maintain emancipation bank account and manage personal income, consistent with your age and developmental level, unless prohibited by the case plan.

- To not be locked in any room, building, or facility premises, unless placed in a community treatment facility.
- To not be placed in any restraining device, unless placed in a postural support and if approved in advance by the licensing agency or placement agency.
- To attend school and participate in extracurricular, cultural, and personal enrichment activities, consistent with your age and developmental level.
- To work and develop job skills at an age appropriate level that is consistent with state law.
- To have social contacts with people outside of the foster care system, such as teachers, church members, mentors, and friends.
- To attend Independent Living Program classes and activities if you are 16 years or older.
- To attend court hearings and speak to the judge.
- To have storage space for private use.
- To review your own case plan if you are over 12 years of age and to receive information regarding out-of-home placement and case plan, including being told of changes to the plan.
- To be free from unreasonable searches of personal belongings.
- To have all your juvenile court records be confidential (consistent with existing law).

Reference: California Code of Regulations—Foster Family Homes Regulations, Section 89372; Group Homes Regulations, Section 84072; Small Family Homes Regulations, Section 83072.

It is VERY important to know the child's rights and explain these rights to each child placed in your care. Doing so will ensure you are not violating any of the regulations and the child(ren) feel empowered.

Identifying Situations Where Abuse May Occur

Child abuse can occur in any situation, regardless of socio-economic status, religion, education, or ethnic background. As a resource parent, you must be willing to inquire into the possibility of abuse. There are four basic areas in which abuse may be revealed:

Environmental

Caregiver Clues

Physical Indicators in the Child

Behavioral Indicators in the Child

This is a partial list of signals that you, as the resource parent, want to be aware of in an effort to protect children.

Environmental could be defined as:

- Hazardous conditions (broken windows, faulty electrical fixtures, etc.).
- Health risks (presence of rats, feces, no running water, no heat, etc.) or unsanitary conditions.
- Extreme dirt or filth affecting health.

Caregiver Clues

- Inability to meet the child's basic needs
- Verbally express thoughts of hurting the child
- Has unrealistic expectations of child (e.g., toilet-training, riding a bike, feeding themselves, etc)
- Singles out one child as "bad" or "evil"
- Berates, humiliates, or belittles child

Physical Indicators in the Child

Physical Abuse

- Unexplained fractures, lacerations, and bruises
- Burns (cigarette, rope, scalding water, iron, radiator)

Neglect

- Malnutrition or poor diet (bloated stomach, extremely thin, or pale)
- Inappropriate dress for weather
- Extremely offensive body odor
- Unattended medical conditions (e.g. infected minor burns, impetigo)

Sexual Abuse

- Bruising, swelling or tearing around genital area, including rectum
- Visible lesions around mouth or genitals
- Complaint of lower abdominal pain
- Painful urination and or defecation

Behavioral Indicators in the Child

Every child responds differently to abuse. There is not one indicator that can clearly be associated with child abuse, although, there may be a number of possible behaviors which can be consistently correlated with abuse. While some of these behaviors occur more with one type of abuse than another, they can overlap.

> The presence of any of these indicators should serve as a warning signal that further investigation may be necessary.

Physical Abuse

- Aggressive behavior toward others; verbally abusive
- Extreme fear or withdrawn behavior
- Destructive—breaks windows, sets fires, etc.
- Out-of-control behavior (angry, panics, easily agitated)

Sexual Abuse

- Engages others in sexualized behavior; promiscuous
- Self-destructiven or self-mutilates
- Pseudo-maturity (seems mature beyond chronological age)
- Eating disorders
- Alcoholism/drug abuse

Neglect

- Clingy
- Self isolation
- Depressed

Emotional Abuse

- Lacks self-esteem; puts self down regularly
- Seeks approval to an extreme
- Unable to make decisions; fears rejection
- Hostile and verbally abusive

Typically children who experience physical and sexual abuse or neglected may also experience emotional abuse; often times these abuses are not isolated.

The most effective way to determine if a child has been abused or is being abused, is to watch how the child behaves. As a mandated reporter, you must stay alert and responsive to the child's behavior.

Children rarely report the abuse while it is happening, but develop coping skills while demonstrating behaviors that may cause attention. Children may also develop a crippling loyalty to their abuser(s) and will often demonstrate a pathological dependency on them.

If you suspect child abuse of ANY kind, listed below are guidelines to determine reasonable suspicion.

Reasonable Suspicion

Means a person can rely on their training or experience
to reasonable suspect child abuse or neglect.
If a mandated reporter has a reasonable suspicion
a child has been abused they have a legal obligation
to report the abuse.

Assessing a child who has the ability to verbally communicate

Two important aspects to keep in mind when interviewing a child who is willing to communicate the situation:

- Create a safe environment
- Create an opportunity for the child to speak freely

Ask the child to describe a typical day and observe the changes in the child's:

- Vocal injections
- Eye Contact and Body movement
- Breathing
- Did the child change the subject abruptly?

Reassure the child you are there to help and it is important they provide detailed information so you can help end the abuse. Be sure to inform the child of your intentions to report the abuse to the Child Protective Service (CPS). You will build trust from the child by keeping him/her informed of your actions during the process.

Assessing a child who is unable to verbally communicate

When children are unable to speak, they may "act out". It is important to assess abuse based on extreme behaviors.

- A child who may have experienced physical abuse may be obsesses with violence and become abusive of dolls as well as animals.
- A child who may have experienced sexual abuse may engage in explicit sexual play and put emphasis on the doll's genitals.

**Although a child obsessed with violence or engages in explicit sexual play may have several meanings, you as a mandated reported should report the incidents so an investigation can be started.
Better to be safe than sorry.

Finally, NEVER guarantee any outcomes to the child. Guaranteeing outcomes could not only ruin your credibility, but could lead to additional disappointments and frustrations.

Good Operating Practices

5

Allowance

All children in placement are entitled to an appropriate allowance. The allowance should be given weekly and may not be withheld for failure to do chores. The allowance given can be spent at the child's discretion. Keep in mind, this is the perfect time to teach the child about money management.

Here is an example of how much to give each child per month based on their age:

AGE OF CHILD	AMOUNT
0-2	$1
3-4	$2
5-7	$3
8-10	$4
11-12	$5
13-15	$8
16-17	$10

Keep in mind, the above chart is only a guide. Use the allowance to teach children money management skills.

Appointments

Medical appointments must be completed within the first three (3) days of a child being placed in your home, when the child was removed from their biological parent's home. The reason this is an important task is so all bruises, broken bones, and other physical signs can be documented. Failure to have a doctor complete a physical could result in you being accused of harming the child.

Some other appointments you will need to schedule include:

- Dental
- Vision
- Therapy
- Family Visits
- Sign-Ups for extracurricular activites, etc.

Boards—Ways to get involved within your community

Review your local Child Welfare Agency to determine which Boards you and your foster youth would like to get involved with. Listed below are a few examples of boards advocating for youth:

- Foster Care Review Boards
- Institutional Review Boards
- Peer Review Boards
- Qualitative Case Review
- Youth Advisory Boards

Child Care

Child care for a foster youth should be provided by a licensed child care provider, however, there is a law regarding Prudent Parenting. (See Prudent Parenting sections for details)

Although this law exist, if the foster child(ren) require consistent and regular care, the resource parent is requried to adhere to the established requirement to hire a licensed care provider. If you have questions, please contact your social worker for clarity.

Children's Records

Children's records are to be kept confidential. No one is to have access to the child's records that is not involved in the case plan. This is important to remember as some information you are exposed to (as resource parent) may be embarrassing to the child if known by anyone else; not to mention sharing the child's information is a violation of their rights. Lets protect the child and his or her information and keep the records locked in a file cabinet.

Clothing / Clothing Allowance

When a child is placed in your home, an initial clothing inventory should be completed for the following reasons:

- To determine what items the child has
- To determine what items the child needs

It is the expectation of the Child Welfare Agency and the Foster Family Agencies that resource parents provide appropriate clothing for each child placed in their home. When a child is initially placed in foster care the police officers and social workers may or may not have had the opportunity to gather all of the necessary clothing for the child(ren), so the social worker will complete the paperwork to get the resource parent a one-time clothing allowance for the child. This inital clothing allowance should be used to obtain the essentials so the child can go to school (if the child is school aged).

Every month the resource parent should purchase clothing and retain the receipts to provide verification of the purchases to the social worker. Another important fact regarding clothing is every piece of article you purchase belongs to the child and should be added to the clothing inventory log. When the child moves placement or is returned home, all of their clothes purhased during their stay with you is to go with them. Do NOT keep their clothes for another child.

**Children over the age of 13 years old should be taught how to spend their clothing allowance in a way to obtain more articles for less. Here is another teaching moment!

Concurrent Planning

Concurrent Planning is a method used to eliminate or minimize delays in obtaining permanency for children in foster care. Once a child has been removed from their biological parent's home and placed in foster care these children are placed with a family that could potentially adopt them.

Of course the goal is to reunify the child(ren) with their parents, however, sometimes the biological parents are unable to care for them. Concurrent Planning not only reduces the amount of time a child remains in the foster care system, but it should reduce the number of moves too.

Cultural Differences

If you have the unique opportunity to parent a child of a different culture then your own, you will have to be prepared to take specific actions to ensure the child feels comfortable.

Some of the first actions you may want to take as a parent, may include:

- Residing in an area where people of your child's race reside
- Attending multicultural activities
- Cooking and eating ethnic meals
- Learning to care for the child's hair and skin (or find someone who can assist you)

- Locate role models with same race for your child to look up to
- Create a positive cultural environment in your home

Keep in mind, not everyone is sensitive to cultural diversity. You may encounter bias. Be sure to handle the topic of culture carefully so the child becomes comfortable and embraces the differences instead of view the differences as a negative. Teach your child everyone is unique and celebrate the uniquness instead of being frightened by it.

Developmental Stages

Developmental stages can be a complicated subject as children develop at different rates. What could be perceived as slower development for one child, may be normal development for another. Listed in this section are a few stages and conerns for various ages. The information presented offers you a guide in assisting you in advocating for the cild(ren) placed in your home.

The developmental stages and concerns can be categorized in four groups:

Physical
Social and Emotional
Thinking
Communication

These signs are general in nature. If you have concerns about the child placed in your home, contact the doctor.

First Year Developmental Potential Challenges

Alert the child's doctor if any of the following developmental delays are present:

- Fails to respond to loud noises
- The child is under weight (3x the birth weight)
- Unable to follow moving objects with their eyes
- Unable to support head or sit with assistance
- Unable to push down with legs
- Does not babble
- Seems overly stiff or flops around like a rag doll
- Persistent drainage or eye drainage
- Unable to crawl
- Does not roll over
- Experiences a loss of skills

Tips to promote healthy growth

- Take the child a bath in an upright position
- Spend time playing with the child
- Reassure the child if he/she is scared or begins to cry
- Use a carseat everytime you travel
- Create routines to make life smoother
- Help the child develop trust; follow through
- Set limits and give choices
- Give safe healthy finger foods
- Allow the child to suck a pacifier. Sucking calms children
- Read to the child daily

Second Year Developmental Potential Challenges

Alert the child's doctor if any of the following developmental delays are present:

- Unable to walk
- Unable to speak
- Does not know the use of common household objects
- Unable to follow basic instructions
- Unable to use a utensils
- Unable to drink from a cup
- Unable to walk up stairs
- Unable to push a wheeled toy
- Unable to jump in place, kick a ball or pedal a tricycle
- Experiences a loss of skills

Tips to promote healthy growth

- Give choices
- Teach independence
- Teach the child about the dangers of knives, strangers, animals, cars, and matches/lighters
- Allow the child to take naps
- Set limits and explain why
- Give the child a time warning before transitioning to the next activity
- Be patience and give the child time to learn
- Spend quality time with the child playing games
- Teach the child to use words instead of hurting others
- Help the child communicate his/her feelings
- Help the child through unfamiliar situations
- Practie positive discipline techniques

Strategies for Potty Training and Tantrums

Potty Training

- Start the process when the child exhibits their willingness. There is no exact age for potty training. Let the child guide you.
- To begin, take child to the bathroom every hour
- When the child has an accident, change him/her quickly, so the child does not become comfortable being wet
- Praise the child's effort; Do not reprimand the child for having an accident
- Teach the child the words used for potty training
- Give the child a toy to play with while on the potty chair
- Dress the child in clothing he/she can easily remove
- Show the child the potty steps:
  - Go to the bathroom
  - Pull down pants
  - Sit down
  - Use the bathroom
  - Wipe
  - Pull pants up
  - Flush toilet
  - Wash hands

Tantrum Avoidance

- Get plenty of sleep
- Eat healthy, balanced meals
- Establlish a regular routine
- Allow physical activities, such as riding a tricycle, run, dance, etc
- Have realistic expectations
- Ignore tantrums, whenever possible
- Remain calm
- Teach the child how to express his/her frustration in words

** Third Year Developmental Potential Challenges **

Alert the child's doctor if any of the following developmental delays are present:

- Have difficulty climbing up or down stairs
- Continuous drooling
- Difficulty handling small objects
- Unable to copy of trace a circle
- Unable to understand basic instructions
- Unable to follow basic instructions
- Extreme separation anxiety
- Experiences a loss of skills

Activities that promote healthy growth

- Give choices
- Continue napping in the afternoon
- Set limits
- Use transition time to the next activity
- Go on bike rides
- Throw a ball back and forth
- Go for walks
- Play games with the child
- Teach the child to use words instead of hurting others
- Help the child communicate his/her feelings
- Help the child through unfamiliar situations
- Allow child to dress himself

**Fourth Year Developmental Potential Concerns **

Alert the child's doctor if any of the following developmental delays are present:

- Unable to throw a ball overhand
- Unable to jump in place

- Clingy and or cries during caregivers separation
- Wants to play alone, ignores other children
- Unable to dress themselves
- Lack of self-control; lashes out when angry or upset
- Unable to use three word sentences
- Experience a loss of skills

Activities that promote healthy growth

- Allow more independence
- Use positive reinforcement to encourage your child
- Use mistakes as a learning opportunity
- Create opportunities for the child to be independent
- Continue afternoon naps
- Give transition warnings, so moving from one activity to another is done with ease
- Establish a library with interesting books / take child to the library
- Be patient
- Spend time reading to your child
- Spend individual time with children
- Give your child permission to say no to adults that make him/ her feel uncomfortable
- Allow your child to express and discuss his/her feelings
- Attend interesting events / outings

**Fifth Year Developmental Concerns **

Alert the child's doctor if any of the following developmental delays are present:

- Behaves extremely fearful, timid, and or aggressive
- Easily distracted
- Refuses to respond to people
- Only expresses being sad or unhappy
- Has difficulty eating, sleeping, or using the potty
- Inability to follow two-part commands

- Unable to give first and last name
- Inability to discuss the days events and experiences
- Inability to climb, run, or ride a bicycle
- Difficulty learning letters, numbers and writing name
- Difficulty recognizing difference and similarities
- Difficulty developing friendships with peers
- Unable to brush teeth
- Experiences a dramatic loss of skills

Tips to promote healthy growth

- Teach the rules to board games and play with the child
- Have indepth conversations about the child's day
- Cook and bake with the child
- Teach the child swimming
- Take the child to the zoo and amusement parks
- Teach the child how to clean his/her room
- Discuss physical gender differences; teach proper names for body parts
- Establish a bedtime routine

** Strategies for child safety **

- Know where the child is at all times
- Give the child timelines
- Teach the child to check in
- Supervise the child's activities
- Provide clear instructions on what to do and what not to do
- Childproof your home
- Be sure to keep the child out of the street
- Be sure the child has protective gear when riding a bicycle, skateboard, or scooter

Education

As Kindergarten children, we learn basic mathematics, 1 + 1 = 2, however, for children placed in the foster care system this seemingly simple equation is really not simple at all. Studies have shown children who experience trauma such as, exposure to domestic violence, neglect, abuse and maltreatment, etc., experience negative long-term consequences. Trauma can also be described as excessive moves and or multi-placements after entering foster care. For example:

> A child is initially removed from their biological parent's home and placed in foster care. Due to various reasons, this same child is moved to another home in foster care, then another, then another. Excessive moves may cause a child to feel insecure, scared, and unwanted. These feelings may make it difficult for the child to concentrate on the tasks at hand.

Sadly, statistics reveal children in foster care typically experience multiple placements before acquiring their permanent placements, such as returning home, being adopted or emancipating out of the foster care system. So addressing educational concerns is essential.

Some of the challenges children experience include:

- Completing homework
- Comprehending assignments
- Inability to develop lasting friendships
- Teachers
- Too many absences
- Lower test scores
- Lower grade point average (GPA)

Of course this is not a comprehensive list of challenges children experience; nor do all foster youth experience them. Hopefully this list will provide you with an idea, so you can assist the children placed in their home.

It may appear to some, the educational needs for foster children have been overlooked. Actually there are several laws on the books to ensure the foster youth are getting their educational needs address and these laws include the following Assembly Bills:

AB 490
AB 1933
AB 1909

Feel free to research these laws for more details

AB 490

> Effective January 1, 2004, AB 490 seeks to ensure all California foster children have the opportunity to meet the challenging state pupil academic achievement standards. The goal is to improve academic attainment for foster children by promoting school stability and identifying a clear preference for enrollment in regular public school.

The key components of school responsibilities include:

- Each local education agency must appoint an educational liaison for foster children (Foster Care Liaison)
    - The liaison shall ensure the school properly places the child in correct classes, enrolls the child in new school, ensure all credits are transferred, obtain records and grades, and ensure the child is checked out of previous school. EC 48853.5 (b)(1)
    - Transfers must be processed within two business days of receiving the request. EC 48853.5 (d)(4)(C)

Use the following contact information to obtain the Foster Care Liaison in your area:

Jackie Wong
Educational Options, Student Support, and
American Indian Education Office
California Department of Education
1430 N Street, Suite 6408
Sacramento, CA 95814
(916) 327-5930
(916) 323-6061 Fax
Email: jawong@cde.ca.gov

- School stability—Allowing the child to remain in school of origin
- In case of disputes regarding school placement, the child has a right to remain in school of origin
- Preference for Regular School Placement unless the child has an Individualized Educational Plan (IEP) which states otherwise. WIC 48853 (a)(1). In addition the person holding the educational rights shall consider placement in regular public school prior to placement in continuation, alternative, or nonpublic schools. EC 48853 (b).
- May request or recommend (in writing) the child be enrolled in any public school based on the residential address, if the move would prove beneficial. EC 48853.5 (d)(2)
- Immediate enrollment even if the foster child is unable to produce academic records, medical records, proof of residency, other documentation or school uniforms. EC 48853.5 (d)(4)(B).
- School must release student records to any county placing agency (including Probation and Child Welfare), without parental consent or court order, for the purpose of fulfilling the requirements of the health and education summary pursuant of Section 16010 of the Welfare and Institutions Code. EC 49076.
- School Credit Calculation—each public school district and county office of education shall accept for credit full or partial coursework satisfactorily completed by the child. EC 48645.5.
- Grade Protection—Schools shall not lower grades of a child in foster care due to absences from school because of a placement

change, court hearing, or other court-related activities. EC 49069.5 (h).

- Diplomas—If the child completes the graduation requirements of the school district, the diploma will be issued by the last school attended before detention occurred. EC 48645.5.
- Foster Caregiver Authority to Consent to IEP Program and Related Services—A foster parent under certain circumstances can consent to Individualized Education Program (IEP) and related services. EC 56055; WIC 366.27; WIC 726.

AB 1933

Approved in September 2010 with the similar goal, yet requires at the initial placement or change of placement, a foster child is allowed to continue his or her education in the school of origin for the duration of the school year.

AB 1909

Foster children: placement: suspension and expulsion: notifications. (established September 2012)

- The educational liaison to notify the foster child's attorney and the appropriate representative of the county child welfare agency of pending expulsion proceedings.
- Authorizes the foster child's caregiver or other person holding the right to make educational decisions for the child to provide the contact information of the child's attorney to the child's school district when the child has been placed outside of the county jurisdiction for the child.
- Authorizes the district superintendent of schools or the district superintendent's designee to invite the pupil's attorney and the appropriate representative of the county child welfare agency to that meeting; using the most cost-effective method possible and notification sent at least 10 calendar days before the date of the hearing.

- Authorizes the health and education summary to include the name and contact information for the educational liaison of the child's local educational agency.

Although many aspects of the foster child's education has been addressed in the Assembly Bills, there still remains the loss of information during and after a traumatic experience, the overwhelming feeling of abandonment, and the devastating realization that one has no control over what is happening to them.

We, as resource parents, need to remember that these children's underperformance may have nothing to do with their IQ scores, but everything to do with the way in which their brain develops.

> It is estimated that a change in placement can result in a foster youth losing an average of four to six months of educational attainment. This is detrimental to the educational process for these children, so excessive moves should be minimized as much as possible.

Becoming an Educational Representative

Becoming an educational representative is vital! You will be in daily contact with the child and will notice the good, bad, and the challenging of the educational process. I recommend the following for anyone becoming an educational representative:

- Keep a detailed journal of all behaviors, reactions, correspondence between you and the school
- Obtain contact information for teacher, principal, and superintendent
- Develop a working relationship with the local foster care liaison
- Attend all scheduled meetings for the child(ren) placed in your care
- Stay in the communication loop
- Ask questions
- Be sure to notify the social worker of any findings

Family Meetings

Family Meetings are defined as a time when all family members come together preferably once a week and consistently. During the meeting, the members decide who will run the meeting, who will keep notes, and who will be the timer. **Keep in mind all members are equal and should not be in trouble for sharing their true feelings.

Family meetings should be used to discuss challenges, weekly schedules, ideas, rules, and what works or doesn't work. Sometimes family members incorporate game playing during their meetings. The goals of the family meeting are:

- To build healthy, strong bonds between family members
- Solve problems in a constructive manner
- Stay up-to-date with schedules
- Share important ideas and information
- Show appreciation

**For some people showing appreciation is uncomfortable, but with practice and consistency you will build stronger family ties.

Family Rules

Family rules are a healthy way to experience harmony within the family unit, establish routines, and create a positive working relationships among its members. One of the main objectives for family rules is to create a sense of involvement and cooperation. When the resource parent allows the child(ren) placed in their home to take an active part in establishing family rules, the child(ren) have a greater sense of belonging. When writing family rules, be sure to write the rules in a positive manner.

Example: Stop running vs. Always walk in the house

Forms

There are numerous forms used to get you through the process of becoming a resource parent, as well as, forms you may need once you've been approved or certified. Listed below are a few of those forms you may want to become familiar with:

STATE OF CALIFORNIA - HEALTH AND HUMAN SERVICES AGENCY

CALIFORNIA DEPARTMENT OF SOCIAL SERVICES
COMMUNITY CARE LICENSING

RECORD OF CLIENT'S/RESIDENT'S SAFEGUARDED CASH RESOURCES

Client/resident: Your signature below indicates you have received the following amount of money from the facility on the date indicated.

Facilities that handle client's/resident's cash resources must maintain accurate records of all money received and disbursed.

INSTRUCTIONS:

1) *The date of the transaction shall be noted under Date.*
2) *Use a separate line for each transaction.*
3) *Supporting receipts for purchases shall be filed in order of dates of purchases.*
4) *The client's/resident's (or client's/resident's representative) signature on this form may serve as a receipt for cash distribution to the client/resident. (Sec. 80026(h)(1)(A) and 87227(g)(1)(A).*
5) *The facility representative's signature is necessary to be able to verify a cash transaction.*

NAME OF CLIENT/RESIDENT:	FACILITY NUMBER:	YEAR

DATE	DESCRIPTION	AMOUNT RECEIVED	AMOUNT SPENT OR WITHDRAWN	BALANCE	SIGNATURE FOR CASH TRANSACTIONS	
					FACILITY REPRESENTATIVE	CLIENT/RESIDENT OR REPRESENTATIVE

LIC 405 (8/01)

STATE OF CALIFORNIA - HEALTH AND HUMAN SERVICES AGENCY

CALIFORNIA DEPARTMENT OF SOCIAL SERVICES
COMMUNITY CARE LICENSING DIVISION

UNUSUAL INCIDENT/INJURY REPORT

INSTRUCTIONS: NOTIFY LICENSING AGENCY, PLACEMENT AGENCY AND RESPONSIBLE PERSONS, IF ANY, BY NEXT WORKING DAY.

SUBMIT WRITTEN REPORT WITHIN 7 DAYS OF OCCURRENCE.

RETAIN COPY OF REPORT IN CLIENT'S FILE.

NAME OF FACILITY	FACILITY FILE NUMBER	TELEPHONE NUMBER
		( )
ADDRESS	CITY, STATE, ZIP	

CLIENTS/RESIDENTS INVOLVED	DATE OCCURRED	AGE	SEX	DATE OF ADMISSION

TYPE OF INCIDENT

- ☐ Unauthorized Absence
- ☐ Aggressive Act/Self
- ☐ Aggressive Act/Another Client
- ☐ Aggressive Act/Staff
- ☐ Aggressive Act/Family, Visitors
- ☐ Alleged Violation of Rights

Alleged Client Abuse
- ☐ Sexual
- ☐ Physical
- ☐ Psychological
- ☐ Financial
- ☐ Neglect

- ☐ Rape
- ☐ Pregnancy
- ☐ Suicide Attempt
- ☐ Other

- ☐ Injury-Accident
- ☐ Injury-Unknown Origin
- ☐ Injury-From another Client
- ☐ Injury-From behavior episode
- ☐ Epidemic Outbreak
- ☐ Hospitalization

- ☐ Medical Emergency
- ☐ Other Sexual Incident
- ☐ Theft
- ☐ Fire
- ☐ Property Damage
- ☐ Other *(explain)*

DESCRIBE EVENT OR INCIDENT (INCLUDE DATE, TIME, LOCATION, PERPETRATOR, NATURE OF INCIDENT, ANY ANTECEDENTS LEADING UP TO INCIDENT AND HOW CLIENTS WERE AFFECTED, INCLUDING ANY INJURIES

PERSON(S) WHO OBSERVED THE INCIDENT/INJURY

EXPLAIN WHAT IMMEDIATE ACTION WAS TAKEN (INCLUDE PERSONS CONTACTED)

LIC 624 (4/99)

OVER

STATE OF CALIFORNIA - HEALTH AND HUMAN SERVICES AGENCY

DEPARTMENT OF SOCIAL SERVICES
COMMUNITY CARE LICENSING

CENTRALLY STORED MEDICATION AND DESTRUCTION RECORD

I. CENTRALLY STORED MEDICATION

INSTRUCTIONS: *Centrally stored medications shall be kept in a safe and locked place that is not accessible to any person(s) except authorized individuals. Medication records on each client/resident shall be maintained for at least one year.*

FACILITY NAME

FACILITY NUMBER

NAME (LAST FIRST MIDDLE)	ADMISSION DATE	ATTENDING PHYSICIAN	ADMINISTRATOR

MEDICATION NAME	STRENGTH/ QUANTITY	INSTRUCTIONS CONTROL/CUSTODY	EXPIRATION DATE	DATE FILLED	DATE STARTED	PRESCRIBING PHYSICIAN	PRESCRIPTION NUMBER	NO. OF REFILLS	NAME OF PHARMACY

LIC 622 (3/99) (CONFIDENTIAL)

STATE OF CALIFORNIA–HEALTH AND HUMAN SERVICES AGENCY

CALIFORNIA DEPARTMENT OF SOCIAL SERVICES
COMMUNITY CARE LICENSING

INSTRUCTIONS:

When reviewing client/resident records in a facility, enter an ✓, x, N/A or complete the space with other appropriate response.

- ✓ - Document required for facility category is complete and current.
- x - Document is lacking, incomplete or requires updating
- N/A - Not applicable

Any item shown as "x" shall be documented on the Licensing Report (LIC 809) with a plan of correction date. File this form in the facility file.

CLIENT/RESIDENT RECORDS REVIEW (RESIDENTIAL)

FACILITY NAME	LICENSE REPORT (LIC 809) DATE
FACILITY NUMBER	TYPE OF VISIT ☐ PRELICENSING ☐ RENEWAL ☐ EVALUATION ☐ COMPLAINT ☐ FOLLOW-UP

*REFERENCE NUMBER	NAME OF CLIENT/RESIDENT	ENTER DATE OF BIRTH	ADMISSION AGREEMENT	ENTER DATE OF ADMISSION	SOURCE OF INCOME	IDENTIFICATION AND EMERGENCY INFO	MEDICAL ASSESSMENT	AMBULATORY STATUS	T.B. TEST	CONSENT FORMS	APPRAISAL AND NEEDS AND SERVICES PLAN	SAFEGUARDS FOR CASH RESOURCES	ENTER INFO REGARDING CASH RESOURCES FROM EACH LEDGER	SAFEGUARDS FOR PROPERTY/VALUABLES	PERSONAL RIGHTS	WEIGHT RECORD	IMMUNIZATION RECORD	CENTRALLY STORED DESTROYED MEDICATION RECORDS	ENTER DATE OF DISCHARGE	COMMENTS
													BAL. DATE							
													BAL. DATE							
													BAL. DATE							
													BAL. DATE							
													BAL. DATE							
													BAL. DATE							
													BAL. DATE							
													BAL. DATE							
													BAL. DATE							
													BAL. DATE							
													BAL. DATE							
													BAL. DATE							
													BAL. DATE							
													BAL. DATE							
													BAL. DATE							

LICENSING EVALUATOR SIGNATURE	DATE

***Reference number corresponds to number used to identify individual client/resident on the field visit report.**

LIC 859 (10/99)CONFIDENTIAL

STATE OF CALIFORNIA - HEALTH AND HUMAN SERVICES AGENCY | CALIFORNIA DEPARTMENT OF SOCIAL SERVICES

AGENCY - FOSTER PARENTS AGREEMENT
Child Placed by Agency in Foster Home

The agreement will be initiated when the child is placed in the facility and whenever the rate changes.

Complete in Duplicate:
One copy to: Foster parents; Child's Social Service Record

NAME OF CHILD		PARENT'S NAME
BIRTHDATE OF CHILD	DATE PLACED	CASE NUMBER
FOSTER PARENT'S NAME		ADDRESS

Anticipated duration of placement is ________ months.

The agency will pay $ __________ per __________ for room and board, clothing, personal needs, recreation, transportation, education, incidentals and supervision. First payment to be within 45 days after placement with subsequent payments no later than the 15th of the month following provision of care.

If additional amounts are to be paid, the reason, amount and conditions shall be set forth here: ____________________

Special problems/needs: ☐ No ☐ Yes If yes, explain ____________________

Special Permissions: Special permission for substitute supervision is subject to Community Care Licensing granting an exception to the licensing regulation, which requires that substitute supervision in the foster home be limited to an adult.

☐ Child 15 years or older has permission to remain without adult supervision during temporary absences of the the foster parent(s), not to exceed six (6) consecutive hours in any one 72-hour period.

☐ Substitute supervision may be provided to the foster child by someone 16 years of age or older (not a foster child) during temporary absences of the foster parent(s), not to exceed six (6) consecutive hours in any one 72-hour period.

☐ Other (Explain) ____________________

☐ No special permissions granted.

AGENCY AGREES TO

1. Provide the foster parent with educational stability requirement, school of origin and travel plan, knowledge of the background and needs of the child necessary for effective care. This may include a social work assessment, medical reports, education assessment, and identification of special needs when necessary. This shall be made available to foster parents within 14 days from date of placement.
2. Develop a plan for the child and share pertinent aspects with the foster parents.
3. Inform foster parents they may give the same consents on behalf of the child as the parent, except for those prohibitions provided in Social Services Manual Regulations.
4. Not remove the child with less than 7 calendar days written notice unless: the child is physically or psychologically endangered; court orders removal; parents or guardians order removal (voluntary placement); signed waiver obtained from foster parents; removal is from an interim placement directly into an adoptive home.
5. Involve foster parents in future planning for the child. The placement shall be reviewed within 6 months.
6. Assist the child in his use of foster care.
7. Assist in the maintenance of the child's constructive relationships with parents and other family members and to involve parents in future planning for this child.
8. Provide procedure for grievances of foster parents.
9. Contact the child and foster parents at least once a month. If case plan would indicate less frequent contacts, the foster parent will be informed.
10. Inform foster parents if child has any tendencies toward dangerous behavior.
11. Provide Medi-Cal card or other medical coverage at time of placement. Arrange for medical examination within 30 days unless child has had such within past 6 months and information is available.
12. Provide a clothing allowance as permitted to meet initial clothing needs.
13. In cooperation with foster parents arrange for visiting by parents or relatives on: ____________________
14. Provide arrangements for school of origin travel as appropriate.
15. Provide assistance with emergencies. Telephone number for after-hours or weekends is: ____________________

***See Next Page for Optional Long-Term Placement Intent**

FOSTER PARENTS AGREE TO

1. Provide this child the nurture, care, clothing and training suited to his needs.
2. Develop an understanding of the responsibilities, objectives, and requirements of the Agency in regard to the care of this child.
3. Recognize the Agency's responsibility for planning for this child, as given by the court or the parent(s).
4. Recognize any limitations of consent imposed by the court or the parent.
5. Increase their knowledge and ability to care for this child.
6. Encourage the child's relationships with his parents and relatives.
7. Cooperate in visiting arrangements between child and parents.
8. Not use corporal punishment, punishment in the presence of others, deprivation of meals, monetary allowances, visit from parent, home visits, threat of removal or any type of degrading or humiliating punishment, and to use constructive alternative methods of discipline.
9. Respect and keep confidential information given about the child and his family.
10. Immediately notify agency of significant changes in this child's health, behavior, or location.
11. Accept the child's special problems as given above in my provision of care.
12. Help with termination of placement including return to his own parents, relatives home, or adoptive placement.
13. Give the agency prior notice of at least 7 days if removal of child is requested unless it is agreed upon with the agency that less time is necessary.
14. Conform to the licensing/certification requirements.
15. Provide state and federal agencies access to documentation when documentation is maintained on children in their care.
16. Give advance written notice to the licensing agency and the person or agency responsible for the child of any (foster parent(s)) absence of 48 hours or longer. (Absence may be reported by telephone in case of emergencies.)
17. Notify the agency immediately if an application is made on behalf of this child for any kind of income. Examples of income include, but are not limited to, child support payments, Veterans Benefits, Railroad Retirement, Social Security, RSHDI, and Supplemental Security Income/State Supplemental Program (SSI/SSP).
18. Remit to Department of Public Social Services any income received on behalf of this child while in foster care up to the full cost of board and care plus medical cost. In addition, I will cooperate to have the Social Security Administration, or the appropriate agency, make the Department of Public Social Services the payee for any funds received on behalf of this child.
19. Foster parent agrees to immediately notify the placing agency of any changes to the child's educational travel, withdrawal from school or graduation.

SOC 156 (12/11) REQUIRED FORM - NO SUBSTITUTE PERMITTED | PAGE 1 OF 2

Print

SUSPECTED CHILD ABUSE REPORT

Reset Form

To Be Completed by **Mandated Child Abuse Reporters**
Pursuant to Penal Code Section 11166

PLEASE PRINT OR TYPE

CASE NAME: ______
CASE NUMBER: ______

A. REPORTING PARTY
NAME OF MANDATED REPORTER | TITLE | MANDATED REPORTER CATEGORY
REPORTER'S BUSINESS/AGENCY NAME AND ADDRESS Street City Zip | DID MANDATED REPORTER WITNESS THE INCIDENT? ☐ YES ☐ NO
REPORTER'S TELEPHONE (DAYTIME) ( ) | SIGNATURE | TODAY'S DATE

B. REPORT NOTIFICATION
☐ LAW ENFORCEMENT ☐ COUNTY PROBATION ☐ COUNTY WELFARE / CPS (Child Protective Services) | AGENCY
ADDRESS Street City Zip | DATE/TIME OF PHONE CALL
OFFICIAL CONTACTED - TITLE | TELEPHONE ( )

C. VICTIM One report per victim
NAME (LAST, FIRST, MIDDLE) | BIRTHDATE OR APPROX. AGE | SEX | ETHNICITY
ADDRESS Street City Zip | TELEPHONE ( )
PRESENT LOCATION OF VICTIM | SCHOOL | CLASS | GRADE
PHYSICALLY DISABLED? ☐ YES ☐ NO | DEVELOPMENTALLY DISABLED? ☐ YES ☐ NO | OTHER DISABILITY (SPECIFY) | PRIMARY LANGUAGE SPOKEN IN HOME
IN FOSTER CARE? ☐ YES ☐ NO | IF VICTIM WAS IN OUT-OF-HOME CARE AT TIME OF INCIDENT, CHECK TYPE OF CARE: ☐ DAY CARE ☐ CHILD CARE CENTER ☐ FOSTER FAMILY HOME ☐ FAMILY FRIEND ☐ GROUP HOME OR INSTITUTION ☐ RELATIVE'S HOME | TYPE OF ABUSE (CHECK ONE OR MORE) ☐ PHYSICAL ☐ MENTAL ☐ SEXUAL ☐ NEGLECT ☐ OTHER (SPECIFY)
RELATIONSHIP TO SUSPECT | PHOTOS TAKEN? ☐ YES ☐ NO | DID THE INCIDENT RESULT IN THIS VICTIM'S DEATH? ☐ YES ☐ NO ☐ UNK

D. INVOLVED PARTIES
VICTIM'S SIBLINGS: NAME BIRTHDATE SEX ETHNICITY | NAME BIRTHDATE SEX ETHNICITY
1 ______ 3 ______
2 ______ 4 ______
VICTIM'S PARENTS/GUARDIANS:
NAME (LAST, FIRST, MIDDLE) | BIRTHDATE OR APPROX. AGE | SEX | ETHNICITY
ADDRESS Street City Zip | HOME PHONE ( ) | BUSINESS PHONE ( )
NAME (LAST, FIRST, MIDDLE) | BIRTHDATE OR APPROX. AGE | SEX | ETHNICITY
ADDRESS Street City Zip | HOME PHONE ( ) | BUSINESS PHONE ( )
SUSPECT:
SUSPECT'S NAME (LAST, FIRST, MIDDLE) | BIRTHDATE OR APPROX. AGE | SEX | ETHNICITY
ADDRESS Street City Zip | TELEPHONE ( )
OTHER RELEVANT INFORMATION

E. INCIDENT INFORMATION
IF NECESSARY, ATTACH EXTRA SHEET(S) OR OTHER FORM(S) AND CHECK THIS BOX ☐ *IF MULTIPLE VICTIMS, INDICATE NUMBER:* ______
DATE / TIME OF INCIDENT | PLACE OF INCIDENT
NARRATIVE DESCRIPTION (What victim(s) said/what the mandated reporter observed/what person accompanying the victim(s) said/similar or past incidents involving the victim(s) or suspect)

SS 8572 (Rev. 12/02)

DEFINITIONS AND INSTRUCTIONS ON REVERSE

DO NOT submit a copy of this form to the Department of Justice (DOJ). The investigating agency is required under Penal Code Section 11169 to submit to DOJ a Child Abuse Investigation Report Form SS 8583 if (1) an active investigation was conducted and (2) the incident was determined not to be unfounded.

WHITE COPY-Police or Sheriff's Department; BLUE COPY-County Welfare or Probation Department; GREEN COPY- District Attorney's Office; YELLOW COPY-Reporting Party

JV-220 Application Regarding Psychotropic Medication

Clerk stamps date here when form is filed.

To keep other people from seeing what you entered on your form, please press the Clear This Form button at the end of the form when finished.

Fill in court name and street address:

Superior Court of California, County of

Fill in child's name and date of birth:

Child's Name:

Date of Birth:

Clerk fills in case number when form is filed.

Case Number:

Attach a completed and signed JV-220(A), *Prescribing Physician's Statement—Attachment,* with all its attachments, must be attached to this form before it is filed with the court. Read JV-219-INFO, *Information About Psychotropic Medication Forms,* for more information about the required forms and the application process.

1. Information about where the child lives:
   a. The child lives ☐ with a relative ☐ in a foster home
      ☐ with a nonrelative extended family member
      ☐ in a regular group home ☐ in a level 12–14 group home
      ☐ at a juvenile camp ☐ at a juvenile ranch
      ☐ other *(specify)*: ______________________________

   b. If applicable, name of facility where child lives: ______________________________

   c. Contact information for responsible adult where child lives:
      (1) Name: ______________________________
      (2) Phone: ______________________________

2. Information about the child's current location:
   a. ☐ The child remains at the location identified in ①.
   b. ☐ The child is currently staying in:
      (1) ☐ a psychiatric hospital *(name)*: ______________________________
      (2) ☐ a juvenile hall *(name)*: ______________________________
      (3) ☐ other *(specify)*: ______________________________

3. Child's ☐ social worker ☐ probation officer
   a. Name: ______________________________
   b. Address: ______________________________
   c. Phone: ____________________ Fax: ____________________

4. Number of pages attached: ______

Date: ____________________

______________________________ ▶ ______________________________

Type or print name of person completing this form *Signature*

☐ Child welfare services staff *(sign above)*
☐ Probation department staff *(sign above)*
☐ Medical office staff *(sign above)*
☐ Caregiver *(sign above)*
☐ Prescribing physician *(sign on page 3 of JV-220(A))*

Judicial Council of California, www.courtinfo.ca.gov
Revised January 1, 2008, Mandatory Form
Welfare and Institution Code, § 369.5
California Rules of Court, rule 5.640

Ask the social worker for clarity. (See Chapter 15: Copies of Frequently Used Forms)

Foster Parent Association

Local

There are many local associations and the contact information appears to change with every newly elected President, so I suggest you contact the State Foster Parent Association to obtain the most current information for your area. See County Contact section for contact information of local Human Service Agencies.

The key is to get involved and find out the latest challenges, most recent updates, and network with other resource parents.

You are not alone! Get involved!

State

The California State Foster Parent Association was established in 1972 by a group of Foster Parents in San Francisco. The main focus is to address issues of Foster Parents, guardianship, adoptive parents, and kinship placements. You can join the state association through your local association, which will send $15 for your membership. If you want to know where the nearest association is, you may call the Membership Chairperson. For additional information log into the following website:

www.csfpaonline.org

National

National Foster Parent Association
2021 E. Hennepin Avenue #320
Minneapolis, MN 55413-1769

Phone: 800-557-5238
Fax: 253-238-4252
Website: http://www.nfpaonline.org/

Membership in the National Foster Parent Association is open to anyone who believes in the importance of family-based care for foster children and that every child deserves a permanent family. NFPA delivers . . . .

- Information
- Advocacy
- Education
- Support

And the opportunity to attend the yearly Foster Parent Conference. Get plugged in and stay involved. Fostering children is serious business. Find out the most current information and meet other resource parents with similar goals.

Grievance Procedure

Grievance procedure is defined as a process one takes when they are dissatisfied with a decision, a placement, or removal of a child placed in their home. The grievance process varies with different family foster agencies and county agencies, so it is important you receive the grievance process with the agency you plan to partner with. Some of the general grievance procedures components include:

- Put your grievance in writing as soon as possible
- Keep a copy for your records
- Submit as appropriate according to your agency requirements

Become familiar with the grievance process before you need it.

Honeymoon Period

The Honeymoon Period is defined as a period of time where the children are on their best behavior trying to make a good impression. Sometimes this period will last a few hours, a few days or a few weeks. Whatever the length of time you experience "happy, happy, joy, joy" do not be fooled or frustrated when the child appears to have a sudden change of heart. The child's actions and attitude may demonstrate his/her unwillingness to cooperate. Be patience and know this period of time is normal and should be handled with care. Believe me, the young person is testing you to determine your true motives. The child(ren) want to know:

Will you support, love, and continue to provide a safe environment for me to live (inspite of how I treat you).

In the child's mind, resource parents take kids into their homes for the money. They want to determine your reason for taking them into your home.

Once the "Honeymoon Period" is over, some children may continue to test your patience, but continue to focus on the end result—which is to care for the children until the permanency plan has been determined.

> The sad truth is many resource parents contact their social worker and put a 7-day notice into the agency / county to have the child removed from their home due to disruptive behaviors.

You need to understand, this transitional period happens with all of the children in foster care. The length of time and severity of the behavior varies, but stay encouraged . . . . these children need you!

**If you can show the young person you are committed to them for the long haul, you will have a successful placement.

Journaling equates to Observing, Recording, and Reporting

The act of journaling is one of those good operating practices to implement when caring for children because journaling will allow you to make an accurate report to the social worker, as well as, determining if there is a pattern of behavior that may need addressing.

When journaling, follow these steps:

1. Observe the behavior
2. Record the situation using the following

    - What happened that causes you concerns?
    - What happened just before the child displayed the concerned behavior?
    - What was your response to the child after the incident?
    - How did the child respond to your response?
    - Where did the incident take place? (Date/Time)
    - What action was taken?

3. Report information to Social Worker, Counselor, Attorney, etc.

Be as detailed as possible.

Your journaling will assist the entire team with important information that can make the child(ren) in your care feel more secure. You will also be able to use the information gathered to address any challenges or encourage the positive behavior during the family meetings.

Liability Insurance

Some states require prospective resource parents show their current homeowner's or renter's insurance to ensure the policy will cover specific damages caused by or to a foster child living in your home. Some states' foster parent associations offer policies specifically for resource families, children and homes.

Check your local association, social worker, and current insurance carrier.

Sample Policy Coverage includes:

- Protection in the event a foster child in your care is injured and you are sued by the child's biological parents or guardian.

- Protection from claims for bodily injury or property damage to the person or property of another because of an act by your foster child.

- Personal injury liability coverage for such things a libel, slander, false arrest, wrongful eviction and alienation of the affection of your foster child from his/her parent.

- Incidental malpractice liability coverage for your failure to provide needed medical care, therapy, diet or other special needs of your foster child.

- Contemplating coverage for foster children under the age of 18 years old

Liability Insurance is definitely a good idea, but check your local area to determine if necessary.

Life Book

Life books are one of the most creative methods for capturing a child's life from the beginning of the foster care process through to the permanency plan. Life books have the following benefits:

- Makes the child the star of the book
- Helps the child understand the processes they are going through
- Give the child a true sense of self
- Captures basic information that often gets lost
- Captures special events, highlight birthdays, sporting events
- Addresses family diversity

- Provides a place to post photos and stories that will help the child understand who he/she is

You can start taking photos of the child when he/she arrives to your home, the child's room, the front of the school, and anything you believe will be important for the child to know.

**It may be a good idea to make two books. Sometimes the child may destroy is or her copy when angry.

Mandated Reporting

The first child abuse reporting law in California was enacted in 1963. The early laws mandated only physicians to report physical abuse. Over the years, numerous amendments have expanded the definition of child abuse and the persons required to report.

According to California's Child Abuse Mandated Reporter Training, the following professions are considered mandated reporters:

- Public assistance workers
- Employees of a child care institution
- Firefighters
- Physicians, surgeons, psychiatrist, dentist, resident, intern, podiatrist, chiropractor, licensed nurse, dental hygienist, optometrist
- Emergency medical technicians or paramedics
- State or county public health employee
- Coroner
- Medical Examiner
- Commercial film and photographic print processor
- Child visitation monitor
- Animal control officer or humane society officer
- Teacher
- Instructional / Teacher's Aide
- Classified employee of any public school
- Administrative Officer or supervisor of child welfare and attendance, or a certified pupil personnel employee

- Administrator of a public or private day camp
- Administrator or employee of a public or private youth center, youth recreation program or youth organization
- Administrator or employee of a public or private children's organization
- Employee of a county office of education
- Licensing worker
- Employee of a school district police or security department
- Any person who is an administrator or counselor
- District attorney investigator, inspector or family support officer
- Licensed nurse
- Nursing students
- Medical students
- Social worker
- Marriage, family and child counselor / trainee
- Clergy member
- Custodian of records of a clergy member
- Probation officer or parole officer
- Peace officer
- Employee of the police department
- Employee or volunteer of a Court Appointed Special Advocates program
- Licensee and administrator or employee of a licensed community care or child day care facility
- Caregivers who work with children with developmental disabilities

When you attend a Mandated Reporter Training, the topics this training will cover include:

- How the law defines child abuse and neglect
- What the law requires of you as a mandated reporter
- What protections the law provides for a mandated reported
- How to spot evidence of child abuse
- How to report child abuse
- What happens after a report is filed
- Definitions of some of the terms used in this program

Procedures for reporting categories of child abuse have also been clarified. In California, certain professionals are required to report known or suspected child abuse. Other citizens, not required by law to report, **may** also do so.

It is important for practitioners and other mandated reporters to keep updated on periodic amendments in the law. Your local Child Abuse Prevention Council or Child Protective Agency has current reporting law information.

Mandated Reporter Frequently Asked Questions

Why Must You Report?

The primary intent of the reporting law is to protect the child. Protecting the identified child may also provide the opportunity to protect other children in the home. It is equally important to **provide help for the suspected abuser**. The report of abuse may be a catalyst for bringing about change in the home environment, which in turn may lower the risk of abuse.

What is Child Abuse?

The Penal Code (P.C.) defines child abuse as: "a physical injury inflicted by other than accidental means on a child by another person." It also includes emotional abuse, sexual abuse, neglect, or abuse in out-of-home care. Child abuse does not include a "mutual affray between minors," "reasonable and necessary force used by a peace officer" under specified circumstances, or spanking that is reasonable and age appropriate and does not expose the child to risk of serious injury. (P.C. 11165.6, Welfare and Institutions Code (W&IC) Section 300.)

What to Report?

The California Child Abuse Reporting Law is found in Penal Code Sections 11165-11174.3. The following is only a partial description of the statute. Mandated reporters should become familiar with the detailed requirements as they are set forth in the Penal Code (P.C.). Under the law, when the victim is a child (a person under the age of 18) and the perpetrator is any person (including a child), the following types of abuse must be reported by all legally mandated reporters:

a. A **physical injury** inflicted by other than accidental means on a child. (P.C. 11165.6).

b. **Child sexual abuse** which includes sexual assault and sexual exploitation. Sexual assault includes sex acts with children, intentional masturbation in the presence of children and child molestation. Sexual exploitation includes preparing, selling or distributing pornographic materials involving children, performances involving obscene sexual conduct and child prostitution. (P.C. 11165.1).

c. **Willful cruelty or unjustified punishment**, which includes inflicting or permitting unjustifiable physical pain or mental suffering, or the endangerment of the child's person or health. (P.C. 11165.3). "Mental suffering" in and of itself is not required to be reported. However, it **may** be reported. Penal Code11166.05 states:

> "Any mandated reporter who has knowledge of or who reasonably suspects that mental suffering has been inflicted upon a child or that his or her emotional well-being is endangered in any other way may report the known or suspected instance of child abuse or neglect to an agency specified in Section 11165.9". (The specified agencies include any police department, sheriff's department, county probation department if designated by the county to receive mandated reports, or the county welfare department.)

d. **Unlawful corporal punishment or injury**, willfully inflicted, resulting in a traumatic condition. (P.C. 11165.4).

e. **Neglect** of a child, whether "severe" or "general," must also be reported if the perpetrator is a person responsible for the child's welfare. It includes acts or omissions harming or threatening to harm the child's health or welfare. (P.C.11165.2).

f. **Any type of abuse or neglect occurring in out-of-home care** (P.C. 11165.5). (For a discussion of newborns with a positive toxicology screen, or for information on child abuse in relation to domestic violence, see the "Questions Often Asked" section.)

When Do You Report?

Child abuse must be reported when one reasonably suspects a child has been the victim of child abuse or neglect . . ." (P.C. 11166(a)).

You must make a report immediately (or as soon as practically possible) by phone. A written report must be forwarded within 36 hours of receiving the information regarding the incident. (P.C. 11166(a)).

To Whom Do You Report?

The report must be made to the Child Protective Services or probation department (if designated by the county to receive mandated reports) or a police or sheriff's department, not including a school district police or security department. (P.C. 11165.9)

Reports by commercial print and photographic print processors, are to be made to the law enforcement agency having jurisdiction immediately or as soon as practically possible. (P.C. 11166(d)).

Immunity

Those persons legally mandated to report suspected child abuse have immunity from criminal or civil liability for reporting as required or authorized by the child abuse and neglect reporting law. (P.C. 11172(a)).

Safeguards for Mandated Reporters

No supervisor or administrator may impede or inhibit a report or subject the reporting person to any sanction. (P.C. 11166(g)).

Persons other than those legally mandated to report are not required to include their names when making a report. (P.C. 11167 (e)). Reports are confidential and may be disclosed only to specified persons and agencies (P.C.11167.5).

Liabilities for Failure to Make A Required Report

A person who fails to make a required report is guilty of a misdemeanor punishable by up to six months in jail and/or up to a $1000 fine, or both. (P.C. 11166(b)). He or she may also be found civilly liable for damages, especially if the child-victim or another child is further victimized because of the failure to report.
(Landeros vs. Flood (1976) 17C.3d 399).

Responsibilities of Agency Employing Mandated Reporter

Any person entering employment which makes him/her a mandated reporter must sign a statement, provided and retained by the employer, to the effect that he or she has knowledge of the reporting law and will comply with its provisions (P.C. 11166.5(a)).

Commercial film and photographic print processors and persons employed by child protective agencies as members of the support staff or maintenance staff and who do not work with, observe, or have knowledge of children as part of their official duties are not required to sign such statements. (P.C. 11166.5(a)).

Licensing Requirement

The state agency issuing a license to a person who is required to report child abuse must either send a statement to the licensee which cites reporting requirements and the penalty for failure to report or print the information on all application forms for a license or certificate printed on or after January 1, 1986. (P.C.11166.5(b)(c)).

Feedback to Reporter

After the investigation is completed or the matter reaches a final disposition, the investigating agency shall inform the mandated reporter of the results of the investigation and any action the agency is taking. (P.C. 11170(b)(2)).

Medications

Whether the child's medication is over-the-counter or perscribed by a doctor, it is vital the medication prescribed to the child is administered exactly as the doctor has prescribed.

In addition to ensuring the medication is administered correctly, be sure to lock the medication in a cabinet out of reach of children in an effort to keep children safe.

> I saw a segment on Good Morning America which talked about teenagers taking the prescription drugs from the medicine cabinets and either selling them to their peers and or using the medication to get high. There has been a few instances where the young person had to be rushed to the hospital due to overdose.

> It is our goal to keep children safe and reduce the number of children selling drugs and or getting addicted to prescription medication, so properly storing the medication will be key.

If you have any questions about what medication to store out of reach of children, look for the "Keep out of reach of children" label. When storing the medication be sure there is a lock on the cabinet and the key is stored in a separate place.

Medical Insurance

All foster youth upon entering the child welfare system is provided medical insurance through the state Medi-Cal program. Medi-Cal is changing their coverage due to budget cuts; however, for foster youth the program will cover all of the essential needs such as; physicals, eye exams, dental, and any referrals for special services. The key is to locate a physician that will take the insurance as payment prior to a child being placed in your home.

Once a child is placed in your home, you will receive a temporary Medi-Cal card until the permanent card arrives. Be sure to keep the card in a safe place and readily accessible so the child placed in your care can be seem by a physician whenever needed.

Permanency

Establishing permenancy for children placed in foster care is essential. It is believed, children need to obtain permanency as quickly as possible to ensure the child has adult connections that will last a lifetime. All to often, children emancipate from care and have no where to go for holidays, spring breaks, or just because.

If children do not establish a connection early, they may become disconnected, which in turn could result in depression. Establishing this connection is vital for the health and welfare of the young person.

Something to consider:

> How many of you turned 18 years old, went off to college or to start a life away from home and never went back? Although there may have been some people to do this, not many.

For this reason, we as resource parents need to make sure the child(ren) placed in our home feel welcomed, safe, secured and an important member of the family.

Prudent Parenting

Senate Bill 358, authorizes a caregiver to arrange for occasional short-term babysitting of their foster child(ren) without requiring the babysitter to undergo any of the requirements, such as, background check, child abuse index check, health screening or CPR training.

Although having all caregivers participate in the screening process will provide you added protection.

Respite Care

Respite care is defined as a temporary short-term placement of your foster child. Using respite care is a great way to relieve stress. For example:

If a child is placed in your home with challenging behavior and you realize your patient level is not 100%, or you have an emergency and are unable to take the child with you, or you made plans for you and your significant other for a weekend get-a-way, or maybe you need time for self-care; whatever your reason, you have the option of placing the child in respite care with someone who has also gone through a similar certification process.

This is the most effective way of taking care of yourself as well as the children placed in your home. Be sure to network with other foster parents when you attend trainings. You can build a dynamic team to assist you during challenging times.

Routines

Routines are a great way to ensure tasks are completed, time is managed successfully, and children know what to expect. When a child is placed in your home be sure to schedule some time to sit down and explain to the child what your family routines are and how you are going to incorporate their activities into your schedule.

Sex and Birth Control

Sex is a topic that makes many parents uncomfortable. So discussing it with young people has almost become non-existence. It is important you move beyond the embarrassment you may feel and reach from deep within yourself and discuss this subject anyway. Keep in mind, it is never too early to have a discussion about sex and birth control.

> I had a 13 year old girl who was eight months pregnant with her first child in one of my parenting classes. When I asked her how she knew about sex, she mentioned her friends. Obviously her friends provided her with inaccurate information.

For this reason resource parents need to provide this vital information to the children placed in our home.

Sexual intercourse can take many forms. The key is to ask the youth their definition of sex, then elaborate, if necessary. (Keeping the conversation age appropriate.) There are numerous books about sex and how to talk to your child. Research, read it, then explain the topic so the youth can understand.

There are numerous birth control methods available, but none of these methods will prevent pregnancy 100%. Listed below are some birth control methods:

Condoms	The Pill
Skin Patch	Ring
Diaphragm	Intrauterine Device (IUD)
Cervical Cap/Shield	Spermicidal Foam
Sponges	Gels

Whichever method one decides to use, be sure to research the advantages and disadvantages of each method to determine the best contraceptive for each person. Also be mindful to discuss the decision with your social worker to be sure everyone involved has all the needed information and any permissions needed can be obtained.

Telephone

The use of the telephone is not only a priviledge, but it is a right. If the child placed in your home wishes to contact his / her lawyer, social worker, or other designated personnel involved in the case plan, they have the right to do so. If the child wants to contact biological parents, friends, etc. these calls need to be in the case plan or approved prior to the child making contact.

Be sure to check with the social worker prior to providing the child with his / her own cell phone. The key is to stay in compliance with the laws established for the case.

Toilet Training

Bye! Bye! Diapers, Hello Dry Pants!

As a parent to young children, I remember looking forward to no longer purchasing a bag of diapers every week for my little bundles to wear in an effort to keep their clothes from soiling.

As a resource parent, it is very important to not pressure the child(ren) into toilet training. Some foster youth have a difficult time with this task due to the trauma they experienced and may need more time to adjust to their new situations. Keep in mind, there is no specific age toilet training should start or be completed by. Society pressures say the child should be potty trained by two years old. Stay focused on your child and wait until he/she is ready.

Listed below are 10 steps to ensure the toilet training process is not only successful, but productive too!

1. Determine if your child is ready for the toilet training experience

2. Determine your readiness for the toilet training experience

3. Purchase the right training equipment i.e. potty chair, pull-ups, pants that can be easily removed, toys, etc.

4. Include the child in the choosing and purchasing process

5. Explain and demonstrate the toilet training process to the child

6. Establish a routine

7. Answer the child's questions

8. Be patient

9. Encourage and praise the accomplishments

10. Celebrate . . . . you and your child did it!

Key Point:

> Children are ready for this process at varying times, so be sure to look for readiness before starting. This first and intial step will reduce frustration for both you and your child.

Transportation

You must provide transportation for every child placed in your home to all necessary appointments. If there is a conflict in your schedule and you are unable to provide the transportation, it is your responsibility to make the necessary arrangments to ensure your child meets all of their monthly obligations. You have a couple of options to ensure each child arrives to their scheduled appointments timely:

- Contact someone in your support system to see if they are willing and able to assist you

- Contact the social worker assigned to your case and see if he / she can assist you

Be sure to have only the amount of children placed in your home that you can take care of. For example, if you reside in a large home and have room for four children, be sure you will be able to get them to and from scheduled appointments, pick them up from day care timely, and be organized enough to keep track of all of their behaviors, actions, and concerns.

Self-Care

6

This section is very important.

Often times as caregivers we fail to take care of ourselves because we are caring for everyone else. We fail to give ourselves the necessary time and attention to be sure we are okay.

Read this chapter and incorporate as many of the techniques into your lifestyle.

- Stress Management
- Support System
- Time Management
- Training

Stress Management

Stress management is another topic of great importance as people are experiencing an enormous amount of stress on a daily basis. The first step to managing your stress is to identify the source(s) of your stress. Stress can come from variest areas in our lives, such as your employment or unemployment, your family, your lack of time to complete specific tasks, unpaid bills, school, deadlines, or just simply too much to do. Stress is defined as an emotional, mental, or physical strain on ones being that may result in depression or anxiety, if not managed properly.

> Regardless of where your stress derives from, the art of managing it will allow you to live a more harmonious life.

Listed below are tips to reducing or preventing stress, as well as, ways to nurture yourself.

- Value yourself and realize your importance. Learn to say "No!"—Be in control of your time.
- Be flexible
- Think positive
- Surround yourself with positive and productive people
- Add a balanced diet, regular exercise, and adequate sleep to your everyday routine
- Establish goals
- Use a calendar to keep record of commitments and due dates
- Plan for fun and relaxation everyday.
- Breakdown large projects into smaller, manageable tasks

Now, lets look at ways to nurture yourself:

- Sing in the shower or the car
- Take naps
- Meditate and/or pray
- Keep a daily journal
- Take a bubble bath while listening to easy listening music
- Close your eyes and take deep breaths

- Write poetry
- Take long walks
- Bake or cook your favorite meal
- Gardening
- Take care of a pet
- Watch your favorite movie or television program
- Post a quote that inspires you on your mirror, where you can see it everyday
- Send a letter to a good friend
- Set realistic goals
- Read, read, and read

Of course you may have additional ways to manage your stress and nurture yourself. This list is to give you ideas, a starting point. Regardless of the activities you decide to use, the point is to make it happen. Find time throughout your day to take care of yourself so you can better care for the children placed in your home.

Support System

A support system is a network of personal or professional contacts available to provide practical or moral support when needed.

It is vital that you have a support system established to assist you in caring for the child(ren) placed in your home. A support system could include neighbors, babysitters, teachers, friends, coaches, clergy, other family members, and anyone that can assist you with dropping off and picking up the child from activities, school or counseling.

**Make developing this list of supporters a priority prior to having children placed in your home. Completing this step first will make the child's transition and you and your family's transition a much smoother process. Keep in mind, the number of supporters in your circle is not important.

Time Management

Time management is defined as scheduling your time to meet the demands of life. When you start thinking about making additions to your household, managing your time in an effort to meet the needs of the household members becomes an important factor.

During my time of training potential resource parents, we discussed time management as an important factor in meeting the needs of the children. Keeping track of your current household member's schedules and your schedule may be a daunting task. Now think about adding a foster child and all of the activities and appointmetns the child may have. i.e. educational needs (Individual Educational Plan (IEP) meetings, tutoring), medical and dental appointments, counseling sessions, family visits, extracurricular activities, friend's activities, social events, and Independent Living Program activities for foster youth 16 years old and older.

Now you can see why time management is of the essence. In order for you to make a positive impact in a child's life you need to have the time for them.

Training

Training is the acquiring of knowledge and skills that will result in acquiring information to assist them in their job as a resource parent. The pre-training classes for resource parents may consist of the P.R.I.D.E training curriculum.

Parents'
Resource for
Information
Development
Education

According to the PRIDE training guide, PRIDE is a model for the development and support of resource families. It is design to strengthen the quality of family foster care and adoption services by providing a standardized, structured framework for recruiting, preparing, and selecting resource parents and adoptive parents. It also provides resource parent in-service training and on-going professional development.

The PRIDE Program has established five (5) essential competency categories which include:

- Protecting and nurturing children;
- Meeting children's developmental needs and addressing developmental delays;
- Supporting relationships between children and their families;
- Connecting children to safe, nurturing relationships intended to last a lifetime;
- Working as a member of a professional team.

After researching many foster family agencies and county departments, the average pre-training hours required for certification range from 9 to 27 hours.

Informing potential parents about the challenges, requirements, and expectations prior to placing a child in the home could result in minimal moves for the foster youth. If your foster family agency or county office does not put emphasis on training . . . . look for a new agency.

Valuable Training Topics

7

The Post-Training subjects for Resource Parents may consist of the following: (Alphabetical Order)

College Planning

Learning how to plan for college is a serious undertaking that must be considered a priority for all youth entering the foster care system. Getting a plan in place, regardless of the child's age, is key to preparing the child for future success. Some of the topics you need to learn about when preparing your young person for college includes:

- Financing your college education
- How to choose the right college
- How to determine what type of college you need to attend
- What classes need to be taken
- What type of degree should they get
- Career options

Remember to remain flexible as the plan may need to be adjusted as the child grows and continue to learn about the world in which he/she lives.

Discipline

The topic of disciplining a foster youth may seem difficult. Some people believe corporal punishment, which is defined as physical punishment is the only way to get a child to do what they want them to do. While other people have learned other methods of disciplining that has a more positive outcome. Regardless of your feelings towards corporal punishment, you cannot use this form of discipline on foster youth, nor can you use this form of punishment on your children once a foster youth has been placed in your home.

When handling the subject of discipline, one must not only be creative, but patient. One method may work for one child and that same method will not work for another. I suggest taking a workshop in Positive

Discipline, Nurturing Parenting, or any other program that will provide you with additional tools. The Positive Discipline classes can provide you with additional information to better equip you to handle foster children and your own children.

Education

Once a child is placed in your home you may notice the child is having difficulty in school. There are classes available to teach you how to advocate for youth. It is vital you recognize the challenges the child is experiencing and address these challenges as quickly as possible.

Once you realize your young person is having a challenge learning, here are some options available to you:

Tutor — Someone who will assist the youth individually or in a small group to bring a deeper awareness to a studied subject.

504 — Falls under civil-rights law, is an attempt to remove barriers and allow students with disabilities to participate freely. This plan seeks to level the playing field, so students can pursue the same opportunities as students who do not have a 504 plan.

IEP — Individualized Education Plan is a plan that requires assistance to students with disabilities and allows them to work at their own pace within the classroom.

SST — Student Study Team, which is an intervention plan for students that are not making satisfactory progress. The SST meeting consist of the teacher, an administrator, the parents and a specialist (depending on what the child needs).

Know your rights. Be sure who has the educational rights for the child(ren) placed in your home and keep this person (if other than yourself) in the communication loop.

False Allegations of Abuse in Foster Care

Sometimes a foster youth may make a false allegation against you. This allegation could cause you to unravel. Try to stay focused and be sure to journal everything associated with the situation. I recommend you:

- Cooperate with the investigators, social workers, and anyone invovled in the investigation.
- Learn the what, where, and when of the situation
- Be patient—the truth will prevail
- Keep good records
- Do not worry

If the allegations are true, be forthcoming as soon as possible. If the allegations are false, have your witnesses available for questionings. Keep in mind these children are coming from troubled backgrounds and sometimes believe they need to lash out at the people closest to them in an attempt to be sent home.

Federal / State Tax Guideline

See your state publications for rules and regulations on claiming a foster youth on your taxes. Also contact the Internal Revenue Service (IRS) for additional information:

Phone: 1 (800) 829-1040
Website: www.irs.gov

Feelings: Positive and Constructive

Teaching children to express themselves in a positive and constructive manner is key to helping them transition into various situations. Keep in mind most of these children may not have learned how to express any feeling other than anger, so this is a perfect opportunity to teach them how to express the many other feelings we have.

Gang Involvement

Being aware of gang involvement within your community is important, especially when working with children over ten years old. At a recent meeting I learned some gangs target children as early as eight years old. It is vital you become aware of the colors, signs, and symbols associated with specific groups.

Foster youth are prime targets for people looking for members as foster youths are viewed as not having a connection with their family and may appear to need people to connect to.

Stay informed by contacting the local Gang Unit at the police department in your community to find out when the next training will be held.

Gay, Lesbian, Bisexual, Transgender, & Questioning Youth

The transitionsforyouth.org website has an article titled, "Talking about Gay, Lesbian, Bisexual, Transgender & Questioning (GLBTQ) Teens", where it mentions there are between five and six percent of youth who are gay, lesbian, or bisexual.

This topic is necessary to discuss and understand, so you can convey this information to your foster youth if questioned. Listed below are the definitions:

Straight	A term which refers to being attracted to the opposite sex
Gay	A term which refers to men being attracted to other men
Lesbian	A term which refers to women being attracted to other women
Bisexual	A term which refers to either men or women being attratced to the same or opposite sex as themselves

Transgender	A term which refers to either men or women who feel they are actually a different gender from their anatomies.
Questioning	A term which refers to either men or women who are questioning whether they are gay or bisexual

Regardless of your personal beliefs or opinion about this topic, it is important that we as resource parents teach tolerance for people different than ourselves.

Tolerance is the practice of recognizing people are different and respecting the differences, even when you do not understand. Use this opportunity to gain a better understanding and knock down the walls which may exist.

Healthy Habits

- Get plenty of rest
- Eat balanced meals
- Research topics of importance
- Join a support group for resource parents
- Be flexible
- Exercise

Money Management

Money management is a process of developing a spending plan of your future earnings. It is vital for you to give the children placed in your home the skill of managing their money. Some steps to developing this spending plan inlcudes:

- Establish a short, mid and long term goals
- Get organized
- Keep track of your spending
- Incorporate a savings plan
- Discuss credit, checking accounts, loans, and retirements

Taking the steps necessary to ensure the children placed in your home are aware of their future spending plan will give them a head start for their future.

If you are not familiar with the topic or uncomfortable discussing it with the children, you can connect with resources within your community. Remember it is never too early to start developing a spending plan. Each child is to receive a monthly allowance, so take this time to assist them with a spending plan for their allowance.

Ombudsman

The Ombudsman office is an agency which reviews issues involving youth in foster care. If you have concerns regarding your foster youth, you can contact the Ombudsman office at: 1 (877) 846-1602. You can also file a complaint with this office. Be sure to have the following information gathered so the representative can assist you in a more appropriate manner:

- Document your complaint—This is where you dcument the:
  - What happened?
  - Who was involved?
  - Where did it happen?
  - When did the incident happen?
  - Give as much details as possible.
  - Provide documentation of the information you're providing
- Be mindful of their time
- Be prepared
- Be truthful

Respositioning The Child for Success

8

Repositioning the Child for Success

Repositioning the child for success is not an easy task; nor is it something that can be done by using a cookie cutter model. Repositioning the child for success is the key to improving the child's outcomes after emancipation. Children who have experienced trauma of any kind may have a difficult time putting all of the pieces of their lives together when preparing for adulthood. These children may feel unloved, insecure, unwanted, unworthy of happiness, and could potentially blame themselves for their circumstances. This is where you can make a huge impact. You can encourage the child to love themselves and to allow you to love them.

Currently, foster youth, who emancipate from the foster care system experience discouraging outcomes which include homelessness, incarceration, early pregnancies as well as many may not graduate from high school.

This section will provide you with insight into how you can help each child within your area of influence through the process of preparing for their future.

Remember:

EACH CHILD HAS THE POTENTIAL FOR GREATNESS!
THEY CAN DO IT!
YOUR TASK IS TO GUIDE THEM IN THE RIGHT DIRECTION!

Listed below are the 7 Steps in the Repositioning process:

1. Change Your Prospective
2. Dream Big!
3. Set Goals and Develop an action plan
4. Examine areas in your life that you would like to re-invent (Overcoming obstacles)
5. Determine what is or could potentially cause you FEAR
6. Surround yourself with positive people (Mentoring)
7. Remain flexible (Balanced Lifestyle)

It is important to keep in mind that during the repositioning process, you will encourage the child to keep dreaming. As the child moves closer to their goals, they may decide to make a few changes along the way. This is okay! If you can remember when you made plans and circumstances change, so you made changes as necessary. Encourage them to:

- Perserve
- Be determined
- Be consistent
- Be passionate
- Be enthusiastic
- Be responsible and to NEVER QUIT!

Show your support for their decisions and keep the encouragement coming.

Now, lets take a closer look at each of the 7 steps individually:

1. Change your Prospsective

To begin the process of helping a young person change their perspective, you want to start with focusing on gratitude. (Gratitude is the feeling of being thankful.)

Sometimes when life throws you a curve ball, it's difficult to focus on the good and positive aspects of your life. The key is to focus their attention on the positive qualities and characteristics of their life and the people in it. When you have a traumatized child, you may want to start with the simple ideas, such as waking up in the morning. (Keep in mind you may need to give them ideas to think about to start the process., i.e. the ability to use their hands, their eyes, their legs, etc.)

When you make a list of things you are grateful for you allow your energy to change. Once the energy changes, the attitude changes. This process creates a rippling effect.

Everyone has experienced negative events during their lifetime. Some of these negative events may include a death of a family member, an illness, a loss of a job, a fight with a friend, etc. The key is to change the thought process behind the experience.

God is in control of every aspect of our lives and once we recognize this fact, we can go through the challenges with increased peace. To help propel the youth in the right direction, take the following steps:

- Sit together and give your young person a pad and pencil
- Brainstorm ideas that he / she is thankful for (Write everything that comes to mind)
- Stay open and focused on the task
- Keep a running list and add to this list often

Keep in mind:

It may be difficult for your young person to think of anything positive during this challenging time, living with people they do not know, being removed form their homes, not being able to see their parents, etc.; however, be patient and relaxed during the process. Do not add additional pressure!

Once the child has made a list of everything they are thankful for, use their list to start a dialogue and be sure to share your list too.

Next step:

Have your young person write down adjectives that best describes them. This step will provide you with insight into how they think of themselves, giving you the framework to start changing their prospective.

> **Side Note:** You may want to share your own experience as a young person. Sometimes we have received negative messages growing up. These negative messages were delivered through our parents, teachers, neighbors, extended family, friends, and siblings. The messages could have been

> "you're too thin," "you're too fat," "you're not as smart as your brother/sister," "you're too smart for your own good," etc. Regardless of the negative messages you may have received, you can change your thoughts into more productive ones. **At this point the child needs to know they ar enot alone. Be authentic! Young people know when you're blowing smoke.**

Once this task is complete, ask the youth open-ended questions, such as:

- What incident(s) led you to think these things about yourself?
- Who are the significant persons in your life?
- What makes this person or persons significant?
- If you could change one thing about your life, what would it be?

After the discussion, you may find your young person may need additional assistance processing the information. Seek the assistance from a member of your professional team, unless you are trained in this field. Explain to them the goal of the activity is to help them begin the healing process.

Next step:

Have the child write down all of the positive aspects of their lives. People tend to have problems writing this part, so be prepared to provide the child with information to get them started. i.e you solved a problem with friends, you graduated from high school, you took my advice. (younger children—you brushed your own teeth, you dressed yourself, etc.)

Now once both list have been compiled, ask them to find the positive for evey negative. i.e. I'm too short—I am the perfect size for my height and so on.

Take your time, this step in the process is critical!

We as parents can assist in changing their minds or at the very least increase their awareness of how significant they are. The first step in changing their prospective, is to find the positive in EVERY situation. Yes, I said EVERY situation. If you believe every incident, circumstance, and or situation happens for a reason, then the "bad" or maybe not as comforting situations we experience, will eventually be for our good. We just have to wait and see the results of our labour. Waiting is not always my specialty and the specialty of others because we live in the microwaveable century where everyone wants everything right now; waiting is not an option. However, if we can encourage each young person to focus on the end result, stay positive and realize that every action that is taken now will have a huge impact on their future.

Be adventureous
Think outside the box
Keep an open mind
and
Continue to love them through the process.

2. Dream Big!

You have to know where you want to go before you start taking steps to get there. This is where you think to yourself, if money was no obstacles or boundaries have no limits, where would you like to go, or what would you like to be, or where would you like to live?

Challenge them to think beyond tomorrow and beyond their current community. Keep in mind people generally cannot think outside the box. Their mind generally thinks as far as their parents have gone or people they respect has ventured.

Examples of some dreams people have told me about:

- Traveling to Italy
- Running a marathon
- Writing a book
- Learning to dance

Assure them their dreams, regardless how big or small, are important.

3. Set Goals and Develop an action plan

Setting goals can be a useful tool that will allow you to experience a more fulfilling life. There are many areas of your life that need goals established. These areas include:

- Attitude
- Career
- Education
- Family
- Finances
- Physical
- Social

You may find there are additional areas you want to establish goals. Do not limit yourself. The above areas will be discussed in this book; however, if you want to add please feel free to do so. The more areas you establish goals, the more fulfilling your life will become.

Goal setting is defined as a means of measuring performance and ensuring a more productive future.

Your task is to assist the child in this process. Take a look at the listed areas where setting goals will be beneficial.

Attitude

Setting goals to change or adjust our attitudes can be the most difficult of all task. Making the necessary adjustments to our attitude could perpel us into new heights and make accomplishing other goals possible.

An example of a needed attitude adjustment:

> I wanted to climb the corporate ladder and fulfill all of my expectations doing so. During this time, I became frustrated, angry and irritable. For many reasons, I could not get ahead. Performing a job that did not allow me to stretch to my full potential proved asinine. Once I realized my destiny, my attitude changed and I started to feel more productive and appreciated.

Make sure when you talk to your young person about the attitude goal setting, take caution. Sometimes people may be on the defense and not willing to recognize their undesirable attributes. Keep the conversation focused on the positive!

Career

Career goals are important for one to obtain the ideal job. The actions you take now will affect your future.

Ask yourself:

- Where you want to be in the next five years?
- How will you get there?
- Do you need a higher level of education?
- What skills do you need to acquire to meet your career goals?
- Do you need more experience?

Keep in mind, people may have three careers during their lifetime. Getting started is the key. If you change your mind, do some research regarding the change, then change. Do not spend alot of time pondering if the change is good or bad. You could be wasting valuable time and energy.

Education

Setting educational goals may first begin with the desire to obtain a degree. Be specific in regards to the type of degree and or certificate you desire, which college will be the best choice in obtaining the type of desired degree or certificate and how much the educational obtainment will cost? Once you start viewing education as a journey you may find more enjoyment with the educational process and be less concerned with education as a destination.

I have vowed to be a lifetime learner. Initially, I wanted to obtain a 4 year degree, then a Masters, then a Doctorate. During my educational journey I decided to take a break after a year into my doctorate degree program and started learning for the sake of learning. As I came across various different subjects, I began researching them for clarity and the idea of being able to discuss with different people. I now enjoy learning, so I encourage people to further their education after they have met their initial goal.

Family

Setting goals for your family will include how much time you desire to spend with them? What type of activities you want to participate in? What type of family traditions do you want to incorporate? If you desire to expand your family and if so when? Do you plan to get married? If so, how old would you like to be when you walk down the isle? This list can go on and on. The more specific you have these goals the more attainable the goals will be.

Finances

Knowledge of finances / money management is the key to a successful financial future. Keep in mind you are in complete control. Trust your instinct! Be patience. Live within your means. (Learning to live within your means will be key to your success.) Decide if you want to purchase a house, car, life insurance, health insurance, invest in a 401K, and or increase your savings, etc. Be sure to meet ALL of your needs before you try and obtain your wants.

Physical

Do you want to lose or gain weight? Do you want to build muscle? Do you want to lose a dress (shirt) size? Whatever your physical personal goals are you should consult a physician prior to setting and starting your weight management journey.

Now, start with taking your measurements from head to toe. Once you have all of the numbers, decide what you would like to do. For example:

I decided I wanted to lose weight. Once I took my measurements, I started walking on the treadmill for 15 minutes. When I was no longer breathing heavy I increased my time and speed. You should look at this process as life changing and change unproductive habits slowly. Be patient and consistent! Focus more on your size than weight as muscle weighs more than fat and looking at your scale can be discouraging at times.

Social

Experience time for self, for family and for friends. Having alone time can assist you with problem solving skills, patience, and prove you with more energy to handle the day-to-day challenges more effectively. Spending time with family will assist in increasing your bonds and develop a deeper connection. Spending time with friends will allow you to relax and release steam.

Keeping a balanced life will allow you to experience life instead of just letting life happen. It is important to reduce frustration and to have a more balanced way of living, to include every aspect of your life

TAKE ACTION!!!

Analyze your unique qualities, strengths, and areas of challenge to determine what you do well and what areas you may need more development.

Determine what is or could potentially cause you fear

False

Evidence

Appearing

Real

I have learned over the years that people typically become paralyzed because of their fear and this fear enables movement. Fear can take many forms. I personally felt the fear of rejection, fear of success, fear of change, fear of my dreams not coming to past, etc. How does one get past their fears?? Just do it! Take each day

Move into your destiny

Now, before you can assist in repositioning a child for success, you first need to understand the child's history. Being aware of where and what has happened to the child is key to knowing the next steps to take. Ask the following questions:

- Was the child living with one or both parents?
- How old is the child?
- Does the child have siblings? If so, how many?
- Did the child experience sexual abuse? Physical abuse? Emotional maltreatment? Chemical dependency? And or Neglect?

Like I mentioned earlier, knowing the experiences of the child can assist you in determining the necessary services needed to help the child process any negative experiences.

Secondly, once a child is placed in your home you will be required to protect and nurture the child so he or she can grow up in an abuse free home. Children need to be free from hurt, harm or danger with established routines that can assist in building trust.

The key to repositioning the child for success is assisting the child in looking beyond their current circumstances and focus on improving. This will not be an easy undertaking. Some children have experienced so much trauma it is difficult to get past it. Remind them of the people who have overcome adversity such as Oprah and Tyler Perry. Informing the children placed in your home of people who overcame their own personal circumstances will allow them to visualize overcoming theirs.

Community Programs

9

Community Programs and Organizations

There are numerous community programs throughout the State of California. The purpose of this section is to highlight a few programs and or organizations that have made a positive impact on foster youth over the years:

California Youth Connection (CYC)

According to the California Youth Connection website (www.calyouthconn.org) CYC is a youth led organization that develops leaders to transform the foster care system throgh policy changes. Check the above website for additional information and to see how you can get involved.

CASA (Court Appointed Special Advocate)

The National CASA Association is a network of programs that recruit, train, and support volunteers to represent the best interests of children placed in foster care. To find out more information and to see how you can get involved, review the following website (www.casaforchildren.org).

Independent Living Program (ILP)

According to the Child World's website (www.childsworld.ca.gov) the Independent Living Program (ILP) provides training and services to assist current and former foster youth achieve self-sufficiency. To find out about the trainings and services they offer review the above website.

Girls Inc.

According to the Girls, Inc's website (www.girlsinc.org) Girls, Inc is an organization that inspires all girls to be strong, smart and bold.

This organization is an excellent resource for young ladies needing to be encouraged, empowered, and supported. Please review the above website to determine how you can assist your little girl obtain current information and support.

Guardian Scholar

The Guardian Scholar program is designed to assist scholars who have faced abuse and neglect. This program is established on the college campuses to make transition into college an easier undertaking. Take a look at the following website to obtain additional information. (www.guardianscholars.com)

John H. Chafee Foster Care Independence Program

The John H. Chafee Foster Care Independence Program was named after Senator Chafee of Rhode Island. This program promotes stability, provides up to $5,000 per year for post secondary education and allows tribes to recive funds to directly administer services. Review the following website (www.nrcyd.ou.edu/chafee) for additional information.

Transitional Housing Program

According to the California Department of Social Services the Transitional Housing Program (THPP) is a housing program for emancipated foster youth at least 18 years old up to their 24th birthday. The goal of the program is to help participants emancipate successfully by providing a safe environment for youth while earning skills that can make them self-sufficient.

Participants may live alone or with a roommate in apartments or single-family dwellings with regular support and supervision provided by THPP staff.

Supportive services include:

- Educational guidance
- Employment counseling
- Assistance reaching emancipation goals outlined in a participant's Transitional Independent Living Plan (TILP)
- Active participants in the independent Living Program

California County Contacts

10

County Welfare and Social Service Directory

Alameda County Department of Children and Families 24100 Amador Street, 5th Floor Hayward, CA 94577 (510) 670-9765 www.alamedasocialservices.org	Calaveras County Children/Adult Services— St. Charles Place 509 E. St. Charles Street San Andreas, CA 95249-9701 (209) 754-6576 www.calavaresgov.us
Alpine County Children's Program 75-A Diamond Valley Road Markleeville, CA 96120 (530) 694-2235 www.alpinecountyca.gov	Colusa County Child Welfare Services 251 E. Webster Street Colusa, CA 95932 (530) 458-0250 www.countyofcolusa.org
Amador County Social Services 10877 Conductor Blvd. Sutter Creek, CA 95685 (209) 223-6651 www.co.amador.ca.us	Contra Costa County Children and Family Services 40 Douglas Drive Martinez, CA 94553 (925) 313-1500 www.cccounty.us/ehsd
Butte County Adult/Children's Services P.O. Box 1649 Oroville, CA 95965 (530) 538-7883 www.buttecounty.net/dess	Del Norte County Social Service Branch 880 Northcrest Drive Crescent City, CA 95531 (707) 464-3191 www.co.del-norte.ca.us

El Dorado County Child Welfare 3057 Briw Road, Ste A Placerville, CA 95667 (530) 642-7300 www.edcgov.us/HHSA	Imperial County Department of Social Services 2995 S. 4th Street, Suite 105 El Centro, CA 92243 (760) 337-6800 www.co.imperial.ca.us
Fresno County Child Welfare Services 2135 Fresno Street, Suite 100 Fresno, CA 93721 (559) 600-2301 www.co.fresno.ca.us/humanservices	Inyo County Adult & Children's Social Services 162 Grove Street Bishop, CA 93514 (760) 873-6533 www.inyocounty.us
Glenn County Protective Services 420 E. Laurel Street P.O. Box 611 Willows, CA 95988 (530) 934-6514 www.hra.co.glenn.ca.us	Kern County Child Protective Services 100 E. California Avenue P.O. Box 511 Bakersfield, CA 93302 (661) 631-6551 www.co.kern.ca.us/dhs
Humboldt County Social Services 929 Koster Street Eureka, CA 95501 (707) 441-5400 www.co.humboldt.ca.us	Kings County Child Welfare Services 1400 W. Lacey Blvd., #8 Hanford, CA 93230 (559) 582-3241 www.countyofkings.com/hsa/index
Lake County Child and Family Services 15975 Anderson Ranch Parkway P.O. Box 9000 Lower Lake, CA 95457 (707) 262-4504 www.co.lake.ca.us	Marin County Children and Family Services 20 N. San Pedro Road, Suite 2028 San Rafael, CA 94903 (415) 473-6924 www.marincounty.org

Lassen County Child and Family Services 1445 Paul Bunyan Road Susanville, CA 96130 (530) 251-8277 www.co.lassen.ca.us	Mariposa County Department of Social Services P.O. Box 99 Mariposa, CA 95339 (209) 966-2000 www.co.mariposacounty.org
Los Angeles County Department of Public Social 12860 Crossroads Parkway South City of Idustry, CA 91746-3411 (562) 908-8400 www.dpss.lacounty.gov	Mendocino County Child Welfare Services 727 South State Street P.O. Box 839 Ukiah, CA 95482 (707) 463-7823 www.co.mendocino.ca.us/hhsa
Madera County Child Welfare Services 629 E. Yosemite Madera, CA 93638 (559) 662-8300 www.madera-county.com	Merced County Department of Social Services 2115 Wardrobe Avenue P.O. Box 112 Merced, CA 95340 (209) 385-3000 www.co.merced.ca.us
Modoc County 120 North Main Street Alturas, CA 96101 (530) 233-6501 www.co.modoc.ca.us	Neveda County Child Welfare Services P.O. Box 1210 Neveda City, CA 95959 (530) 265-1340 www.mynevedacounty.com
Mono County Children Services P.O. Box 2969 Mammoth Lake, CA 93546 (760) 924-1770 www.monocounty.ca.gov	Orange County Child and Family Services 888 N. Main Street Santa Ana, CA 92701 (714) 541-7793 www.ocgov.com

Monterey County Family and Children's Services 1000 S. Main Street, Suite 216 Salinas, CA 93901 (831) 755-4448 www.mcdses.co.monterey.ca.us	Placer County Children's Services 11716 Enterprise Drive Auburn, CA 95603 (530) 889-6778 www.placer.ca.gov/hhs
Napa County Child Welfare Services 2261 Elm Street Napa, CA 94559-3721 (707) 253-4279 www.countyofnapa.org	Plumas County Social Service Department 270 County Hospital Road Suite 207 Quincy, CA 95971 (530) 283-6350 www.countyofplumas.com/ socialservices
Riverside County Children's Services 4060 County Circle Drive Riverside, CA 92503 (951) 358-3000 www.dpss.cp.roverside.ca.us	San Diego County Child Welfare Services 1600 Pacific Highway Room 206 MS P501 San Diego, CA 92101-7439 (858) 616-5812 www.sdcounty.ca.gov/hhsa
Sacramento County Child Protectives Services Foster Care 700 H. Street #7650 Sacramento, CA 95814 (916) 875-1590 www.sacdhhs.com	San Francisco County Family and Children's Service P.O. Box 7988 San Francisco, CA 94120 (415) 558-2660 www.sfhsa.org

San Benito County Child and Adult Services 1111 San Felipe Road #206 Hollister, CA 95023 (831) 636-4190 www.cosb.us	San Joaquin County Children's Services 102 S. San Joaquin Street P.O. Box 201056 Stockton, CA 95201-3006 (209) 468-1000 www.sjgov.org/hsa
San Bernardino County Children and Family Services 385 N. Arrowhead Avenue 5th Floor San Bernardino, CA 92415 (909) 388-0242 www.hss.co.san-bernardino.ca.us/hss	San Luis Obispo County Child Welfare P.O. Box 8119 San Luis Obispo, CA 93403 (805) 781-1600 www.slocounty.ca.gov/dss
San Mateo County Children and Family Services 1 Davis Drive Belmont, CA 94002 (650) 802-7507 www.co.sanmateo.ca.us/portal/site/humanservices	Shasta County Children's Services 2650 Breslauer Way Redding, CA 96001 (530) 229-8400 www.shastahsa.net
Santa Barbara County Child Welfare & Adult Services 234 Camino del Remedio Santa Barbara, CA 93110 (805) 681-4401 www.countyofsb.org/social_services	Sierra County Health and Human Services P.O. Box 1019 Loyalton, CA 96118 (530) 993-6707 www.sierracounty.ws

Santa Clara County Department of Family & Children Services 333 West Julian Street, 5th Floor San Jose, CA 95110 (408) 501-6800 www.sccgov.org/portal/site/ssa	Siskiyou County Social Services Department 818 South Main Street Yreka, CA 96097 (530) 841-2700 www.co.siskiyou.ca.us
Santa Cruz County Family and Children's Services 1000 Emeline Avenue Santa Cruz, CA 95060 (831) 454-4062 www.santacruzhumanservices.org	Solano County Child Welfare Services 275 Beck Avenue—MS 5-200 Fairfield, CA 94533-6804 (707) 784-8331 www.solanocounty.com/depts/hss
Sonoma County Family, Youth, & Children's Department P.O. Box 1539 Santa Rosa, CA 95402-1539 (707) 565-5800 www.sonoma-county.org/human	Trinity County Child Protective Services 51 Industrial Parkway P.O. Box 1470 Weaverville, CA 96093-1470 (530) 623-1265 www.trinitycounty.org/department
Stanislaus County Adult, Child, & Family Services Division 251 E. Hackett Road P.O. Box 42 Modesto, CA 95353-0042 (209) 558-2520 www.co.stanislaus.ca.us/dss	Tulare County Child Welfare Services 5957 South Mooney Boulevard Visalia, CA 93277-9394 (559) 624-8000 www.tularehhsa.org

Sutter County Social Services 190 Garden Highway P.O. Box 1535 Yuba City, CA 95992 (530) 822-7230 www.co.sutter.ca.us	Tuolumne County Child Welfare Services 20075 Cedar Road North Sonora, CA 95370 (209) 533-5718 www.tuolumnecounty.ca.gov
Tehama County Child Welfare Services 310 S. Main Street P.O. Box 1515 Red Bluff, CA 96080 (530) 527-1911 www.tcdss.org	Ventura County Children & Family Services 855 Partridge Drive Ventura, CA 93003 (805) 654-3456 www.ventura.org
Yolo County Children & Adult Services 25 North Cottonwood Street Woodland, CA 95695 (530) 661-2750 www.yolocounty.org	Yuba County Children's Services 5730 Packard Avenue Suite 100 P.O. Box 2320 Marysville, CA 95901 (530) 749-6311 www.co.yuba.ca.us/Departments/HHSD

Informational Websites

10

There are many foster care resources available about foster care on the internet. Listed below are a few you can log onto and research some very important informaton and keep up to date with the current laws and regulations affecting the youth in your care:

www.Advokids.org

www.cacfs.org

www.caichildlaw.org

www.calyouthconn.org

www.casey.org

www.cwla.org

www.FosterCareInfo.org

www.fosteryouthhelp.ca.gov

www.youthlaw.org

Definitions

11

A

Abuse is to use something in an improper, illegal, or harmful way; to treat a person or animal cruelly, whether physically, psychologically, or sexually.

Administrative Review means a review conducted every 6 months per Federal legislation, of children in out-of-home care. The purpose may be to examine an individual case for purposes of permanency planning or may be part of a wider process examining the effectiveness of the system.

Adoption Plan is a formal plan (usually in writing) that is created by one or both of the biological parents of a child who it is planned will be placed for adoption.

Adult is a person 18 years of age or older.

Affidavit is a formal legal document containing written statement of legal significance that are being sworn to under oath by the author of the document.

Aging Out means a youth emancipating from the foster care system after turning 18 years old.

Agreement means a written document signed by two or more persons specifying what each person plans and agrees to do.

Anti-Social Behavior generally refers to actions that deviate significantly from established social norms. Behavior that fits within this definition will vary to some degree, based on the social environment in which the child lives.

Assessment Process is the process of gathering, evaluating, and documenting in the case plan relevant information to the case.

Attention Deficit Disorder (ADD) is the term which describes a lifelong developmental disability that can be detected in infancy, early childhood or even in adolescence, and which affects a child's ability to concentrate and control impulses and behavior.

Attention Deficit Hyper Activity Disorder (ADHD) is the term which describes a lifelong developmental disability that can be first detected in infancy, early childhood or even in adolescence, and which involves challenges with attention span, impulse control, and the intensity of activities at school, home or at work. Typical behavior would include such things as distractibility, difficulty with following instructions or waiting for turns within groups; difficulty staying on task with chores or play activities; difficulty sitting or playing quietly; inattention; restlessness; and engaging in physically harmful or dangerous activities.

B

Behavioral Health is the interdisciplinary study of behavioral, psychosocial, and biomedical knowledge relevant to the understanding of health and illness.

Bipolar Disorder is the term is used to describe a form of mental illnesses in which moods and reactions are affect, and which is characterized by irregular cycles of mania and/or depression. During manic the periods, the affected individual may be in a very elevated mood and exhibit symptoms of hyperactivity, wakefulness, distractibility or even irritability. During the depressive periods, affected individuals can exhibit sustained symptoms of depression, disinterest in most activities, fatigue, sleep disturbance, ranging anywhere from insomnia to hypersomnia, weight loss, weight gain, and sluggish or delayed mental reasoning.

Blow Out of foster care placement is a term used when the child is not getting his/her needs met and must be removed and placed in another home.

Bonding is the process that a child goes through in developing lasting emotional ties with its immediate caregivers, which is seen as the first and most significant developmental task of a human being, and is central to that person's ability to relate properly to others throughout its life.

C

Case Plan means a written document which is developed based upon an assessment of the circumstances which required child welfare services intervention; and a social worker identifies goals.

Case Worker aka Social Worker is the individuals that prepare adoption home studies for prospective adoptive parents, assist prospective adoptive parents in obtaining their pre-adoption certificate, where required, assist in providing post-placement supervision of adoptive families to help them adapt the changes that they undergo in their lives as the result of adoption.

Certified Family Home means a family residence certified by a licensed foster family agency and issued a certificate of approval as meeting licensing standards.

Central Auditory Processing Disorder (CAPD) is the term which describes a condition in which the affected individual whose hearing capabilities are otherwise functionally sound, will have difficulty understanding and processing information that is heard. All of the possible causes of this disorder are not known; however some include head trauma, lead poisoning, and possibly chronic ear infections.

Child means a person under 18 years of age who has not emancipated

Child Abuse means non-accidental injuries against a child. The term includes emotional, physical, and sexual abuse as defined in Section 31-002(c)(7)(A) through (D).

> **Emotional Abuse** means the nonphysical mistreatment, the results of which may be characterized by disturbed behavior, such as withdrawal, regression, bizarre behavior, hyperactivity, or dangerous acting-out behavior.

Physical Abuse means non-accidental bodily injury that had been or is being inflicted on a child.

Sexual Abuse means the victimization of a child by sexual activities, including, but not limited to, those activities defined in Penal Code Section 11165.1

Child Health and Disability Prevention (CHDP) means a public health, well child program to provide health care services and health assessment services to eligible children.

Child in Immediate Danger means a child whose health or safety are in jeopardy as described in Welfare and Institutions Code Section 306(b).

Child Neglect is defined as any recent act, or failure to act, that results in the death of a child, or in an endangerment of a child, or the creation of an imminent risk of the death or serious physical or emotional harm, or sexual abuse of a child.

Child Welfare Services means public social services directed toward protecting and promoting the welfare of children as defined by Welfare and Institutions Code Section 16501(a).

Concurrent Planning is an innovative foster care case management tool that is employed by caseworkers and other child welfare staff members, where they pursue the primary goal of family reunification, while at the same time, they are also developing an alternative permanency plan for the child. This alternative plan will often include adoption as the major alternative to family reunification. If the family reunification efforts fail, then the alternate plan will already be in place and well on its way to completion. Concurrent planning is intended to reduce the total period of time a child will remain in foster care before being permanently placed with a family.

Conduct Disorder is a behavioral condition involving a pattern of repetitive and persistent conduct that infringes on the basic rights of others or does not conform to established societal norms or rules that are appropriate for a child of that age.

Confidentiality is the legally required process of keeping secret; the legally and ethically required principle and practice which compels adoption attorneys, social workers, employees of adoption agencies, court personnel and other professionals to not disclosed identifying or other significant information about the parties to an adoption, without legal authority and the written consent of the involved parties to do so. Also, not available to the public due to sensitive matters

Co-Parenting is a long-term, formal informal, agreement or plan to help provide the necessary support and resources to meet the needs of children.

Counseling means assisting the child and his/her family to analyze and better understand the situation; select methods of problem-solving and identify goals and explore alternatives behaviors.

Court Appointed Special Advocate (CASA) is a nonprofit network supporting and promoting court appointed volunteer advocacy for abused and neglected children so they can thrive in safe, permanent homes.

Crisis Intervention means determining the cause of the crisis; offer support to families, defuse situations; and assess potential harm.

Custodial Parent is a parent that has the legal right to the physical custody of its child, either under the provisions of a state law granting custody, or under the provisions of a court granting custody to one of its parents in preference over the other parent.

D

Day Care defines a child care facility as described by Health and Safety Code Section 1596.750

De Facto is a term meaning "in actual fact," regardless of legal or normative standards, and refers to an action or a state of affairs, which for all practical purposes, must be accepted, but which has no formal legal basis.

Dependent Child is a term generally refers to a child who has been placed in the legal custody of either the state or the county foster care system by the courts, usually due to the abandonment, abuse, neglect of the child by its parents or other caregivers.

Developmental Disability is the term which refers to a severe and chronic impairment, which can be attributed to one or more mental or physical impairments which will require specific and lifelong or extended care that is individually planned and coordinated, and which had an onset before age 22, and which is likely to continue indefinitely. The condition or conditions must create substantial functional limitations in three or more of the following areas of major life activity: **(1)** self care, **(2)** language skills, **(3)** learning, **(4)** personal mobility, **(5)** self-direction, **(6)** potential for independent living, and **(7)** potential for economic self-sufficiency as an adult.

Disruption is the term which generally refers to an adoption that for some reasons has not become final, even though the adoptive parents were identified as the parents to adopt the child and the child may have even been placed in their home for a period of time.

DNA (deoxyribonucleic acid) Testing is the generic blueprint that determines a person's biological characteristics. DNA is located in the cell of the human body. This unique combination of DNA will match that of the biological parents of the child.

E

Education is the imparting and acquiring of knowledge through teaching and learning, especially at a school or similar institution; training and instruction in a particular subject.

Emancipation is the condition or fact of being freed from restrictions. Typically, children turn 18 years old and are released from the care ad control of the child welfare system.

Emergency Response Assessment means an assessment of an emergency response referral conducted by a skilled and trained social worker.

Emotional Disturbance is a severe, pervasive or chronic emotional / affective condition which prevents a child from performing everyday tasks. This condition is characterized by an inability to build or maintain relationships, inappropriate behaviors or feeling under normal circumstances, a pervasive mood of unhappiness or depression, or a tendency to develop physical symptoms or fears related to personal or school problems. Children may require special classrooms and teachers trained to help children with these special needs.

Exploitation means to use unfairly for one's own advantage. Sexual abuse can take the form of child exploitation for example, by photographing the child in compromising situations; kidnapping and selling children into prostitution; or forcing someone younger and weaker to do your will.

Extended Family means the relatives of an individual, both by blood and by marriage, other than its immediate family, such as aunts, uncles, grandparents and cousins.

F

Facilitators are individuals that are not licensed as agencies or attorneys, who engage in either matching birth parents with adoptive parents; or instruct classes on specific subjects.

Family is defined as a group of relatives; people living together; lineage; offspring; or a group with something in common.

Family Maintenance is a division in child welfare that has activities designed to provide in-home protective services to prevent or remedy neglect, abuse, or exploitation, for the purpose of preventing separation of children from their families as per W&I Code Section 16501(g).

Family Preservation is a program that is designed to keep families together by providing support and intervention services to children and families in their home, where the family unit can be observed, evaluated and treated together.

Family Reunification is a program that is designed to provide time-limited foster care services to prevent or remedy neglect, abuse, or exploitation, when the child cannot safely remain at home, and needs temporary foster care, while services are provided to reunite the family as per W&I Code Section 16501(h).

Fetal Alcohol Effect (FAE) is a disorder associated with cognitive and behavioral difficulties in children who birth mothers drank alcohol during her pregnancy.

Fetal Alcohol Syndrome is the term which refers to certain birth defects, and serious, life-long mental and emotional impairments that may be suffered by a child as the result of heavy alcohol consumption by its mother during pregnancy. Symptoms of mental and emotional deficits may include significant learning and behavioral disorder (including attention deficits and hyperactivity), poor social judgment, diminished cause-and-effect thinking, and impulsive behaviors.

Fictive Kin is a term used to refer to individuals that are unrelated by either birth or marriage, who have an emotionally significant relationship with another individual that would take on the characteristics of a family relationship.

Filiation is the condition or fact of being the child of a particular parent, as in the judicial determination of the maternity or paternity of a child.

Finalization Hearing is a court hearing where in most states an adoption becomes final. Usually, the adoptive parents and the child to be adopted go to court with the adoption case worker, and their lawyer if it is an independent adoption, and provide testimony to the court regarding the appropriateness of the adoption.

Foster-Adoption aka "Fost/Adopt" is when a child placement in which birth parents' rights have not yet been severed by the court or in which birth parents are appealing the court's decision but foster parents agree to adopt the child if/when parental rights are terminated.

Foster Care means the 24-hour care and supervision of a child who has been removed from their biological families and placed by a placing agency in one of the following types of foster homes:

- A licensed foster family home
- A family home certified by a licensed foster family agency
- A licensed group home

Foster Children are defined as children that are in the legal guardianship or custody of a state, county, or private adoption or foster care agency, yet are cared for by foster parents in their homes, under some kind of short-term or long-term foster care arrangement with the custodial agency. These children will generally remain in foster care until they are reunited with their parents, or until their parents voluntarily consent to their adoption by another family, or until the court involuntarily terminates or severs the parental right of their biological parents, so that they can become available to be adopted by another family.

Foster Family Agency is defined as an organization engaged in recruiting, certifying, and training potential foster parents to provide 24-hour care and supervision of children in the child welfare system.

Foster Parents are defined as person(s) whose home is licensed or certified through a foster family agency to provides 24-hour care and supervision of a child(ren) placed in the child welfare system.

G

Genealogy is a term referring to the study of family history.

Grief is defined as a deep feeling of emotional loss.

Grievance means an expression of dissatisfaction with a child placing agency's procedures or actions, regarding a placement, care of a child, removal of a child in foster care.

Group Homes are defined as alternative to traditional in-home foster care for children, in which children are housed in an intimate or home-like setting, in which a number of unrelated children live for varying periods of time with a single set of house parents, or with a rotating staff of trained caregivers.

Guardian is defined as a person who fulfills some of the custodial and parenting responsibilities of the legal parents of a child, although the court or biological parents of the child may continue to hold some jurisdiction and decision-making authority over the child.

I

Immediate Family is defined as a term that is generally used to refer to the smallest unit of a family that an individual lives with, which usually includes a father, a mother and siblings; however, an immediate family can be comprised of grandparents, aunts, uncles, etc.

Independent Living Program is a program designed to help provide life-skills training to older foster youth, to assist them to acquire the skills they will need to live independently as adults. These types of programs are designed for children who are "aging out" of foster care, as they near majority, and for whom there is no other plan for permanent adoption placement.

Indian Child Welfare Act of 1978 (ICWA) is a Federal law that takes precedence over the local adoption laws of every state and gives

Native American Indian Nations and Tribes, including the Alaskan Aleuts, the right to control adoptions that involve their tribal members. In any instance where the provisions of any state law might conflict with ICWA, ICWA will always prevail.

Individualized Educational Plan (IEP) is a written plan for educational support services and their expected outcomes, which is developed for students who are enrolled in special education programs.

Inter-Ethnic Placement is a term which refers to placements of children that fall within the coverage provided under Section 1808 of P.L. 104-188 [42 USC 1996b], known as the Removal of Barriers to Interethnic Adoption Act, which affirms the prohibition contained in the Multi-Ethnic Placement Act of 1994, against delaying or denying the placement of a child for adoption or foster care on the basis of race, color, or national origin of the foster or adoptive parents or of the child involved.

Interstate Compact are a set of laws created in the form of a suggested model state statue covering a specific area of law that is of general concern to all states, which is usually drafted by a committee with input from all or a large number of the states.

Interstate Compact on Adoption and Medial Assistance (ICAMA) is a compact that has been adopted by the legislatures of compact member states, which governs the interstate delivery of and payment for medical services and adoption assistance payments and subsidies for adopted children with special needs.

Interstate Compact on the Placement of Children (ICPC) is an interstate compact, or agreement, that has been enacted into law by all 50 states in the United States, and the District of Columbia, which controls the lawful movement of children from one state to another for the purposes of adoption. Both the originating state, where the adoption of the child will take place, must approve the child's movement in writing before the child can legally leave the originating state. This Compact regulates the interstate movement of both foster children and adoptive children.

Irrevocable Consent is a term used to describe a Consent to Adoption that has been signed by the biological parent of a child that is being placed for adoption, which under state law cannot be revoked after it is signed, unless the court specifically finds that the Consent to Adoption was obtained by fraud or misrepresentation, or by the use force or undue duress on the birth parent.

J

Jurisdiction is a legal term referring to the authority or power that a court will have over the individuals or the subject matter of the cases that will appear before it for consideration or decision.

K

Kinship Care is defined as the full-time care and nurturing of a child by someone who is related to the child or by a significant prior relationship connection.

L

Learning Disabilities (LD) is defined as having one or more impairments that a child may have in such areas as reading, mathematics and/or written expression skills, which interfere with the expected academic performance of the child in school, or in other daily activities that require those skills.

Legal Custody refers to a legal relationship that is established by court order, in which one individual, referred to as the Custodian, if given legal authority over, and the corresponding legal responsibility for, the physical care of another individual.

Legal Guardian is a person who has the legal responsibility for providing the care and management of a person who is incapable, either due to age (very young or even very old, or to some other physical, mental or emotional impairment, of administering his or her own affairs.

Legally Free occurs when the rights of a child's biological parents are legally terminated, either by their death, legal consent, or by a forced termination by the court, then the child becomes legally "free" to be adopted by another set of legal parents.

Liability is defined as an obligation under law; legal responsibility for something, especially costs or damages; something for which somebody is responsibly, especially a debt

Liability Insurance is defined as insurance against liability that pays damages where a person or organization is found responsible for injury or harm caused, e.g. in the case of negligence

Licensing Agency is defined as the California Department of Social Services (CDSS) office responsible for the licensing and enforcement of the California Community Care Facilities.

Life Books are pictorial and written representation of the life of a child, which is designed to help the child better understand and make sense of its unique background and history. Although there is no required content for a life book, some information that it might include would be information about birthparents, other members of the extended birth family, birthplace and date.

Long-Term Foster Care is a term that has been used to refer to the intentional retention of a child in foster care for an extended period of time.

Loss is a feeling of emotional deprivation that is experienced when someone or something dies. Loss is also felt by a birth parent when their child is placed in foster care; by adoptive parents who are infertile; an adopted child may feel a sense of loss when he/she realizes he/she is adopted; and a foster child may feel a sense of loss every time he/she is moved from one placement to another. i.e. the loss of schools, friends, neighborhoods, routines, teachers, etc.

M

Mainstreaming is a term that typically refers to the placement of a child with special developmental, physical, emotional or educational deficiencies or challenges into a regular classroom setting for part or all of the school day, with the long-term goal of helping the child make a gradual adjustment into as many aspects of normal life as possible.

Maltreatment is defined as physical abuse, child neglect, sexual abuse, and emotional abuse. Federal CAPTA legislation (P.L. 104-235) provides definitions that identify a minimum set of acts or behaviors that characterize maltreatment.

Mandated Reporter is a person who, pursuant to the Child Abuse and Neglect Reporting Act, is required to report knowledge or reasonable suspicion of child abuse which is obtained while acting in a professional capacity or within the scope of his/her employment.

Matching is the process of bringing together qualified prospective adoptive parents and willing birth parents that are compatible with each other; who can agree on the terms under which the adoptive parents can adopt the available child.

Maternity Home is a group residency environment where a pregnant women who is considering placing her unborn child for adoption can live until her child is born. The women who live in a maternity home may pay a small fee or no fee to live in the home and they often apply for public assistance and Medi-Cal payments.

Mental Health describes a level of cognitive or emotional well-being or an absence of a mental disorder.

Mental Retardation is the impaired or incomplete mental development characterized by an IQ of 70 or below and characterized by significant functional limitations in at least two of the following skills: communication, self-care, home living, social/interpersonal skills, use of community resources, self-direction, functional academic skills, work, leisure, health, and safety. Degrees of severity reflect the level of intellectual impairment:

Mild Mental Retardation	—IQ level 50-55 to approximately 70
Moderate Retardation	—IQ level 35-40 to 50-55
Severe Mental Retardation	—IQ level 20-25 to 35-40
Profound Mental Retardation	—IQ level below 20-25

Mentoring is a developmental relationship between a more experienced individual, a mentor, and a less experienced partner, a mentee. Through regular interactions, the mentee relies on the mentor's guidance to gain skills, perspective, and experience.

Minor means a person under 18 years old

Multi-Ethnic Placement Act is the Federal Act, which was enacted in 1994, is found in P.L. 103-382 [42 USC 622], and prohibits the delay or denial of any adoption or placement in foster care due to the race, color, or national origin of the child or of the foster or adoptive parents, and requires States to provide for diligent recruitment of potential foster and adoptive families who reflect the ethnic and racial diversity of children for whom homes are needed.

Multi-Racial Adoption is a term used to refer to the adoption of children whose family heritage includes more than one race.

N

Neglect is a term to describe something or someone not being cared for properly.

Non-Identifying Information is the health and other family background information which is commonly exchanged or otherwise made available to the other members of the adoption triad, but which does not include identifying information, such as names, addresses, birth dates and telephone numbers.

Non-Recurring Adoption Related Expenses is a term which refers to certain one-time adoption-related expenses, which may be at least partially reimbursed to families adopting children with special needs under state-sponsored adoption assistance programs.

Non-Relative Adoption is a term used to refer to the adoption of a child by adoptive parents who are not biologically related to the child.

Notice of Hearing is the document that contains the details about when and where the adoption finalization hearing will take place. This notice must be delivered or served to all individuals that are legally required to be given notice of the hearing, or properly published in the newspaper for those involved individuals who cannot be located.

O

Occupational Therapy is a type of rehabilitation therapy that uses real life activities in specific areas and with specific goals, to help patients of all ages prevent, lessen, or overcome physical disabilities.

Open Adoption Records is where adult adoptees over a certain age, usually over the age of 21, are able to obtain their original birth certificate without the requirement of a court order.

Open Adoption is where both identifying and non-identifying information about the adoptive parents and the birth parents is shared with each other, which can include last names, addresses, and telephone numbers.

Oppositional Defiant Disorder is a recurrent pattern of negativistic, defiant, disobedient, and hostile behavior toward authority figures that persists for at least six months. This disorder is characterized by frequent occurrence of at least four of the following behaviors: frequent loss of temper, tendency to argue with adults, refusal to obey adult rules or requests, deliberate behaviors to annoy others, spiteful and vindictive behavior, being touchy or easily annoyed by others, being angry and resentful, use of obscene language, and a tendency to blame others for mistakes or misbehaviors.

Orphan is a term which refers to a child who either has no living parents, or whose parents have disappeared or have abandoned the child, or a child who has only one living parent who is not able to adequately provide for the proper care and support of the child.

Orphanage is an institution that houses children who are orphaned, abandoned, or whose parents are unable to care for them.

P

Parens Patriae is a legal term that defines the State's legal role as the guardian to protect the interests of children who cannot take care of themselves.

Parent means the natural or adoptive father or mother, or other adult fulfilling the parental role.

Parental Rights is all of the legal rights, and the corresponding legal obligations, that go along with being the parent of a child, which include: the right to legal and physical custody of the child, the right to physical access or visitation with the child, the right to inherit property from the child and to have the child inherit property from the parent, the right to consent to medical care and treatment for the child, the right to consent to the marriage of the child or its enlistment in military service, the ability to contract on behalf of the child, the obligation to provide financial support for the child, the responsibility to provide a legal defense of the child in legal proceedings, the obligation to care for, direct and supervise the child, the obligation to be legally liable for certain damages caused by the child, the obligation to see that the child attends school, and the obligation to protect the child and provide a safe living environment for the child.

Parenting Training means child development, home management, and consumer education provided through specialized formal training and practice in parenting skill achievement in accordance with Welfare and Institutions Code Section 16507.7.

Paternity Testing (See DNA Testing)

Paternity is the identity of the biological father of a child

Permanency Planning is the systematic process of carrying out a set of goal-directed activities designed to help children live in permanent families.

Petition to Adoption is the document that is filed with the court to commence your adoption action. It states the legal basis on which you think you should be able to adopt this child, why the court has jurisdiction to grant the adoption, your qualifications to adopt this child and the name that you want to be given to your child when the requested adoption becomes final.

Photolisting Book is a publication that contains photos and descriptions of children who are available for adoption.

Placement Date is the date at which the child comes to live with the foster or adopting parents.

Placement is the term used to describe the point in time when your child comes to live with you in your home.

Planning is the process of setting goals, developing strategies, and outlining tasks and schedules to accomplish the goals.

Post-Institutionalized Child is a child adopted from institutional, hospital, or orphanage settings. The term is used to describe an array of emotional and psychological disturbances, developmental delays, learning disabilities, and/or medical problems resulting, in part, from their stay in institutions.

Post-Legal Adoption Service are services provided subsequent to legal finalization of the adoption. There are primarily four types of post-legal service providers; social service agencies, private therapists, mental health clinics and self-help groups.

Post-Reunion Issues are a range of feelings from euphoria to despair possible after the reunion of birth relatives. Family members in reunion may feel a “let down” or a range of feelings including guilt, anger, jealousy, confusion or happiness that may be related to completion of the reunion process and the beginning of a process whereby family members do or do not negotiate an ongoing relationship.

Post-Traumatic Stress Disorder (PTSD) is a condition in which victims of overwhelming and uncontrollable experiences are subsequently psychological affected by feelings of intense fear, loss of safety, loss of control, helplessness, and extreme vulnerability and in children the disorder involves disorganized or agitated behavior.

Post-Adoption Period is a period of time after an adoption is finalized during which the members of this new group of legally related individuals learn together to become a real family unit, with all the joys, challenges, accommodations and wonderful experiences that go with it.

Post-Placement Report is a written report that is prepared for the court in an adoption case by an adoption caseworker that makes a series of personal visits to the home of the adoptive parents. The purpose of these post-placement visits is to observe how well the child and the prospective adoptive parents are bonding to each other and how well the child is fitting into the family.

Preferential Consideration means that the relative seeking placement shall be the first placement to be considered and investigated.

Prenatal Substance Exposure is when fetal exposure to maternal drug and alcohol use which can significantly increase the risk for developmental and neurological disabilities. The effects can range from severe (neurological damage and growth retardation) to minor (resulting in normal outcomes). Infant and child long-term development depends not only on the prenatal exposure (type of drug, amount, length of time of use), but on factors related to the child's own biological vulnerability and environmental conditions.

Pre-Placement Period is the period of time between when a home study or adoption certification is completed for adoptive parents, and when they actually bring home a child that they wish to adopt.

Presumed Father is the individual that the law presumes, until shown otherwise, to be the legal father of a child.

Private Adoption Agency is a licensed agency that may have a non-profit, not-for-profit or for-profit legal and tax status, and can be either general in their scope, or can develop an expertise and focus in a certain type of adoption, such as international adoptions, the adoption of foster children, or the adoption of children with special needs or those with a certain ethnic background.

Psychological Parent is a person whom a child considers to be his or her parent, even though that individual may not be biologically related to the child. A person who fits in this capacity is sometimes called a "de facto" parent.

Public Adoption Agency is a term that refers to a rather broad group of state and county adoption agencies that bear a wide variety of names, depending on the particular provisions of the laws in their state, such as The Department of Human Services, The Department of Social Services, and The Department of Children and Family Services. These agencies are responsible under the provisions of state law for placing waiting children from foster care or other institutional care settings into the homes of adoptive families.

R

Reactive Attachment Disorder is a term used to describe a condition that generally appears in children before age five, and is thought to result from a lack of consistent care and nurturing in early years.

The disorder is characterized by the inability of a child or infant to establish age-appropriate social contact and relationships with others. Symptoms of the disorder may include a failure to thrive, developmental delays, a refusal to make eye contact, feeding difficulties, hypersensitivity to sound and/or touch, failure to initiate or respond to social interactions with others, self-stimulation, discriminate sociability and an unusually high susceptibility to infections.

Re-Adoption Residential Treatment is a term used to describe the practice of adopting a foreign child in the United States after it has already been adopted by its adoptive parents in the foreign country of its origin. The most common reason for a re-adoption is to allow the child to obtain a United States birth certificate, written in English, showing the adoptive parents as though they were the biological parents of the child.

Rebuttable Presumption is an assumption that is made in the law that will stand as a fact unless someone comes forward to contest it and prove otherwise.

Recruitment refers to the process of attracting, screening, and selecting qualified people for a specific job.

Relative means, for purpose of preferential consideration for placement of a minor, an adult who is a grandparent, aunt, uncle, or sibling of a minor.

Relinquishment is the term generally refers to a birthparent voluntarily giving up his or her parental rights to a child, so that someone else can adopt it.

Residential Care Facility is a structured 24-hour care facility with highly-trained staff that provides psychological services to help severely troubled children overcome behavioral, emotional, mental, or psychological problems that have had an adverse affect on their family interactions and relationships, their school achievement, and their peer group relationships and socialization.

Residential Treatment is a therapeutic intervention processes for individuals who cannot or do not function satisfactorily in their own home environments. For children and adolescents, residential treatment tends to be the last resort when a child is in danger of hurting himself or others.

Respite Care is temporary or short-term home care of a child that is provided, either for pay or on a voluntary basis, by adults other than the birthparents, foster parents, or adoptive parents that the child normally resides with, which is designed to give the parents some time away from the child, and even the child some time away from the parents, to allow them to emotionally recharge and become better prepared to handle the normal day-to-day challenges of parenting.

Reunification is the returning of the child to the custody of the biological parents, after the child had been placed in foster care.

Reunification Services are services designed to help get children that are in foster care, and their biological parents, into a position where they can live together again as a family unit.

Reunion is a term used to refer to a personal meeting between an adoptee and one or more of its birth relatives.

Revocation aka "Reversal" is the process by which a birth parent nullifies a Consent to Adopt that he or she previously signed.

Ritalin is a commonly prescribed drug to help to control some of the symptoms of attention deficit disorder (ADD). It may have a calming effect and help to improve concentration.

S

Sealed Adoption Records are the original birth certificate of an adopted person, and records of court proceedings, agency reports, and other documents are sealed to protect the confidentiality of the parties to an adoption.

Search and Consent Procedures are sanctioned under State law, that authorize a public or private agency to assist a searching party to locate another party to an adoption, in order to determine if the party being sought would be agreeable to the release of identifying information about them to the searching party, or would be willing to agree to a personal meeting with the searching party.

Seriously Emotionally Disturbed means those children described in Welfare and Institution Code Section 5600.3.

Semi-Open Adoptions is a form of adoption that is intentionally designed to be a combination of a more traditional closed adoption and a more progressive open adoption, with the emphasis being on the "privacy" of all parties, rather than on "confidentially." Direct communication after the adoption is more limited, in the fashion that is agreed by the parities to be beneficial for everyone.

Severance of Parental Rights aka "termination of parental rights" is the process of involuntarily taking away the parental rights of a parent that has abandoned a child, has without just cause failed to support a child, has neglected or abused a child, has stood by and allowed others to neglect or abuse a child, or who because of extended incarceration in prison, will be unavailable to properly parent or nurture the child during its formative years.

Sexual Abuse is the employment, use, persuasion, inducement, enticement, or coercion of any child to engage in, or assist any other person to engage in, any sexually explicit conduct or any simulation of such conduct for the purpose of producing any visual depiction of such conduct; or rape, and in cases of caretaker or inter-familial relationships, statutory rape, molestation, prostitution, or other form of sexual exploitation of children, or incest with children.

Sexual Abuse Symptomology are indicators and behaviors which suggest that a child may have been sexually abused, including: excessive masturbation, sexual interaction with peers, sexual aggression towards younger and more naïve children, seductive behavior, and promiscuity.

Small Family Home means any residential facility, which provides 24-hour care for six or fewer foster children who have mental disorder or developmental or physical disabilities and who require special care and supervision as a result of their disabilities.

Special Needs generally refers to children that traditionally have been more difficult to place for adoption, because they are older, or have some form of physical, mental, emotional, or developmental challenge, or who are multi-ethnic or bi-racial children. This definition also includes children that are part of a sibling group that it is expected would do better if they were adopted together.

Special Needs Children are children who are emotional or physical disorders, age, race, membership in a sibling group, a history of abuse, or other factors contribute to a lengthy stay in foster care. Common special needs conditions and diagnoses include: serious medical conditions; emotional and behavioral disorders; history of abuse or neglect; medical or genetic risk due to familial mental illness or parental substance abuse.

Speech and Language Disorder means an impairment of speech or receptive language. Speech disorders usually involved difficulties with articulation which can generally be improved or resolved with speech therapy, usually requiring treatment over months or years. Language disorders, on the other hand, often result in substantial learning problems, involving difficulty with language comprehension, expression, word-finding and/or speech discrimination. Treatment by a language therapist generally leads to improvement in functional communication skills, although treatment cannot be generally expected to eradicate the problem.

State Agency means the California Department of Social Services (CDSS)

Statutes are laws, including both state and federal laws

Stepparent Adoption is the adoption of a child by the new spouse of the birthparent.

Substitute Care is any kind of custodial or residential care for a child that is ordered or otherwise sanctioned by the court, and in which a child does not continue to live with either of the birth parents.

Substance Abuse is excessive consumption or misuse of substance for the sake of its non-therapeutic effects on the mind or body; especially drugs or alcohol

Suitability Study is a separate report that is prepared for the court by the adoption caseworker, while in other states it is included as part of the post-placement report that the caseworker prepares for the court. The purpose of this study is to provide the court with a professional evaluation of whether the home of the adoptive parents is a suitable and nurturing place for this child to live and be cared for.

Supplemental Security Income (SSI) is a Federally-funded needs-based disability program for adults and children which provides monthly cash benefits and, in most states, automatic Medicaid eligibility.

Surrender, in the context of an adoption, is a term used to refer to a voluntary, as opposed to an involuntary, termination of parental rights by a biological parent of a child that is to be adopted, when the parent signs a formal written Relinquishment or a Consent to Adoption document, which usually takes place in the presence of witnesses and/or a Notary Public.

Surrender Papers is a legal document attesting to the signator's voluntary relinquishment of parental rights to a child.

Surrogacy Court handles legal matters that in other states would customarily be handled by Probate or Family Court. It handles matters where one individual legally stands in the place of another individual to accomplish a specific legal purpose for a specific period of time. A Surrogacy Court does not have anything directly to do with the type of "surrogacy" arrangements where fertile women act as the carriers of a pregnancy for otherwise infertile couples, where thy become pregnant either by artificial insemination or by an embryo transplant, or other similar procedure.

Surrogate Mother is a woman who carries and gives birth to the child of another woman, who is usually infertile, by way of a pre-arranged legal contract. Surrogacy arrangements have a variety of accompanying legal issues and are not legally permitted or recognized in all states.

System is often referred to as "the public child welfare system." Also refers to the network of governmental organizations providing a range of child welfare services.

T

Tax Exclusion For Adoption Benefits are provisions that are contained in the Internal Revenue Code which allow adoptive parents to exclude from their adjusted gross income for federal income tax purposes, some cash or other adoption benefits that they receive from a qualifying employee benefit plan that has been provided by their employer.

Therapeutic Day Services means non-medial care, counseling, educational, or vocational support, or social rehabilitation services on less than a 24-hour basis to children who would otherwise be placed in foster care.

Therapeutic Foster Home aka "Treatment Foster Home" is a foster home in which the foster parents have received specialized training to enable them to provide care for a wide variety of children and adolescents, usually those with significant emotional or behavioral problems. Parents in therapeutic foster homes are more closely supervised and assisted than parents in regular foster homes.

Tourette's Syndrome is a treatable neurological disorder that consists of involuntary "tic" movements or vocalizations that become more apparent under stress. Common manifestations include shoulder-shrugging, neck-jerking, facial twitches, coughing, grunting, throat clearing, sniffing, snorting, and barking. Children with Tourette's often have problems with hyperactivity as well.

Therapy is treatment of physical, mental, or behavioral problems that is meant to cure or rehabilitate somebody

Transitional Housing Program is a placement opportunity for young adults, who emancipated from the child welfare or probation systems. The goal of the program is to provide a safe living environment while helping them develop the life skills they currently may not have. The program provides supervised transitional living housing and supportive services based on a Transitional Independent Living Plan (TILP). The TILP is developed by the young adult and other supportive persons, and details the goals and objectives he/she will achieve while working towards self-sufficiency.

Transitional Independent Living Plan (TILP) is an agreement designed to capture the goals the youth would like to accomplish over a period of 6 months and allows them to stay focused and keep track of their progress.

Transportation means conveying a child from one place to another when mobility is necessary to support a specific case plan, and no other means of conveyance is available.

Trans-Racial Adoptions is an adoption in which a family of one race adopts a child of another race.

U

Unfounded Report means a report of child abuse, which is determined by a child protective agency investigator to be false, to be inherently improbably, to involve an accidental injury, or not to constitute child abuse, as defined in Penal Code Section 11165.6.

V

Visits are a face-to-face contact between a child and his/her biological family members. i.e. parents, grandparents, siblings, aunts, uncles, and any other persons deemed appropriate by the county or juvenile court.

W

Waiting Children is a term generally refers to non-infant, school age children, who have become legally available for adoption. They will generally be under the legal jurisdiction and care of public foster care agencies, and will have come into the foster care system for a variety of reasons, which could include neglect, abandonment, abuse and/or some other dysfunction within their family environment.

Ward of the Court is defined as the court taking responsibility for the legal protection of a child or someone who is incapacitated.

Wrongful Adoption is an adoption that it is claimed would not have taken place had the adopting parents been properly informed of certain significant information that was known to those that were arranging the adoption at the time that the adoption took place, but which was not disclosed to the adoptive parents. This withheld or undisclosed information can include a variety of things, such as serious physical, emotional or psychological defects or deficiencies.

Bibliography

12

Bibliography

Child Welfare Information Gateway. (2011). Series: Factsheets. Current through 2011. Retrieved August 15, 2011, from: http://www.childwelfare.gov/pubs/otherpubs/majorfedlegis.cfm

The Children's Aid Society. (2011). Foster Care & Accomplishments. Retrieved August 15, 2011, from: http://www.childrensaidsociety.org/adoption-foster-care/foster-care-history-accomplishments

Child Welfare Information Gateway. (1980). Overview. Retrieved August 15, 2011, from: http://www.childwelfare.gov/systemwide/laws_policies/federal/index.cfm?event=federalLegislation.viewLegis&id=22

Nakyanzi, L. (2011). Foster Care System Faces Problems. ABC Primetime. http://abcnews.go.com/Primetime/story?id=132011&page=1

Adoption.com (2011). The Largest Glossary of Adoption-related Terminology. Adoption Glossary. Retrieved August 15, 2011, from: http://glossary.adoption.com/

The Foster Care System. (2011). Foster Parents. Retrieved from: http://library.thinkquest.org/05aug/01584/fosterparents.html

Grimm, B. And Darwall, J. (2005). Foster Parents: Who Are they and What Are Their Motivations? Retrieved from: http://www.youthlaw.org/publications/yln/2005/july_september_2005/foster_parents_who_are_they_and_what_are_their_motivations/

Thomas, R. (1999). Children Abused in Foster Care. Retrieved from: http://www.angelfire.com/co2/childprotectorwatch/FCabuse.html

Patton, V. (2009). Woman gets 2 years for abusing child. Retrieved from Merced Sun Star from: http://www.mercedsunstar.com/2009/08/21/1014275/woman-gets-2-years-for-abusing.html

Thoma, R. (2003). A Critical Look At the Foster Care System: Incentives to Foster Parents. Retrieved from: http://www.liftingtheveil.org/foster07.htm

2010 Report to the Legislature and the Governor for the Foster Youth Services Program. (2010). Retrieved from: http://www.cde.ca.gov/ls/pf/fy/documents/legreport2010.doc

Clay, R.A. (2010). Treating Traumatized Children. Retrieved from: http://www.apa.org/monitor/2010/07-08/children.aspx

California Department of Sociak Services. (2011). Transitional Housing. Retrieved from: http://www.childsworld.ca.gov/PG1353.htm

Pennell, J., Shapiro, C., and Spigner, C. (2011). Center for Juvenile Justice Reform. Safety, Fairness, Staility: Repositioning Juvenile Justice and Child Welfare to Engage Families and Communities. Retrieved from: http://cjjr.georgetown.edu/pdfs/famengagement/FamilyEngagementPaper.pdf

The Formalization of Foster Care. (2008). Retrieved from: http://www.faqs.org/childhood/Fa-Gr/Foster-Care.html

American Colossus: The Triumph of Capitalism, 1865-1900, by H.W. Brands, 2010. Retrieved from: http://www.childwelfare.gov/systemwide/laws_policies/federal/index.cfm?event=federalLegislation.viewLegis&id=42

Summary of The Adoption and Safe Families Act of 1997. Retrieved from: http://library.adoption.com/articles/summary-of-the-adoption-and-safe-families-act-of-1997.html

Ashe, Nancy. (2003). Insurance for foster parent. Retrieved from: http://www.fosterparenting.com/foster-care/insurance-for-foster-families.html

National Association of Social Workers. (2003). Keeping Children and Families Safe Act of 2003. Retrieved from: http://www.naswdc.org/advocacy/updates/2003/030503.asp

Child Welfare Information Gateway. (2006). Safe and Timely Interstate Placement of Foster Children Act of 2006. Retrieved from: http://www.childwelfare.gov/systemwide/laws_policies/federal/index.cfm?event=federalLegislation.viewLegis&id=82

Children Defense Fund (2012). Fostering Connections to Success and Increasing Adoptions Act. Retrieved from: http://www.childrensdefense.org/policy-priorities/child-welfare/fostering-connections/

John Burton Foundation. (2014). California Fostering Connections to Success. Retrieved from: http://cafosteringconnections.org/

Copies of Frequently Used Forms

15

STATE OF CALIFORNIA - HEALTH AND HUMAN SERVICES AGENCY

CALIFORNIA DEPARTMENT OF SOCIAL SERVICES
COMMUNITY CARE LICENSING

RECORD OF CLIENT'S/RESIDENT'S SAFEGUARDED CASH RESOURCES

Client/resident: Your signature below indicates you have received the following amount of money from the facility on the date indicated.

Facilities that handle client's/resident's cash resources must maintain accurate records of all money received and disbursed.

INSTRUCTIONS:

1) *The date of the transaction shall be noted under Date.*
2) *Use a separate line for each transaction.*
3) *Supporting receipts for purchases shall be filed in order of dates of purchases.*
4) *The client's/resident's (or client's/resident's representative) signature on this form may serve as a receipt for cash distribution to the client/resident. (Sec. 80026(h)(1)(A) and 87227(g)(1)(A).*
5) *The facility representative's signature is necessary to be able to verify a cash transaction.*

NAME OF CLIENT/RESIDENT:	FACILITY NUMBER:	YEAR

DATE	DESCRIPTION	AMOUNT RECEIVED	AMOUNT SPENT OR WITHDRAWN	BALANCE	SIGNATURE FOR CASH TRANSACTIONS: FACILITY REPRESENTATIVE	CLIENT/RESIDENT OR REPRESENTATIVE

LIC 405 (8/01)

STATE OF CALIFORNIA - HEALTH AND HUMAN SERVICES AGENCY

CALIFORNIA DEPARTMENT OF SOCIAL SERVICES
COMMUNITY CARE LICENSING DIVISION

UNUSUAL INCIDENT/INJURY REPORT

INSTRUCTIONS : NOTIFY LICENSING AGENCY, PLACEMENT AGENCY AND RESPONSIBLE PERSONS, IF ANY, BY NEXT WORKING DAY.

SUBMIT WRITTEN REPORT WITHIN 7 DAYS OF OCCURRENCE.

RETAIN COPY OF REPORT IN CLIENT'S FILE.

NAME OF FACILITY	FACILITY FILE NUMBER	TELEPHONE NUMBER ( )
ADDRESS	CITY, STATE, ZIP	

CLIENTS/RESIDENTS INVOLVED	DATE OCCURRED	AGE	SEX	DATE OF ADMISSION

TYPE OF INCIDENT

☐ Unauthorized Absence	Alleged Client Abuse	☐ Rape	☐ Injury-Accident	☐ Medical Emergency
☐ Aggressive Act/Self	☐ Sexual	☐ Pregnancy	☐ Injury-Unknown Origin	☐ Other Sexual Incident
☐ Aggressive Act/Another Client	☐ Physical	☐ Suicide Attempt	☐ Injury-From another Client	☐ Theft
☐ Aggressive Act/Staff	☐ Psychological	☐ Other	☐ Injury-From behavior episode	☐ Fire
☐ Aggressive Act/Family, Visitors	☐ Financial		☐ Epidemic Outbreak	☐ Property Damage
☐ Alleged Violation of Rights	☐ Neglect		☐ Hospitalization	☐ Other *(explain)*

DESCRIBE EVENT OR INCIDENT (INCLUDE DATE, TIME, LOCATION, PERPETRATOR, NATURE OF INCIDENT, ANY ANTECEDENTS LEADING UP TO INCIDENT AND HOW CLIENTS WERE AFFECTED, INCLUDING ANY INJURIES

PERSON(S) WHO OBSERVED THE INCIDENT/INJURY

EXPLAIN WHAT IMMEDIATE ACTION WAS TAKEN (INCLUDE PERSONS CONTACTED)

LIC 624 (4/99)

OVER

STATE OF CALIFORNIA - HEALTH AND HUMAN SERVICES AGENCY

DEPARTMENT OF SOCIAL SERVICES
COMMUNITY CARE LICENSING

CENTRALLY STORED MEDICATION AND DESTRUCTION RECORD

I. CENTRALLY STORED MEDICATION

FACILITY NAME

INSTRUCTIONS: *Centrally stored medications shall be kept in a safe and locked place that is not accessible to any person(s) except authorized individuals. Medication records on each client/resident shall be maintained for at least one year.*

FACILITY NUMBER

NAME (LAST FIRST MIDDLE)	ADMISSION DATE	ATTENDING PHYSICIAN	ADMINISTRATOR

MEDICATION NAME	STRENGTH/ QUANTITY	INSTRUCTIONS CONTROL/CUSTODY	EXPIRATION DATE	DATE FILLED	DATE STARTED	PRESCRIBING PHYSICIAN	PRESCRIPTION NUMBER	NO. OF REFILLS	NAME OF PHARMACY

LIC 622 (3/99) (CONFIDENTIAL)

STATE OF CALIFORNIA–HEALTH AND HUMAN SERVICES AGENCY

CALIFORNIA DEPARTMENT OF SOCIAL SERVICES
COMMUNITY CARE LICENSING

CLIENT/RESIDENT RECORDS REVIEW (RESIDENTIAL)

INSTRUCTIONS:
When reviewing client/resident records in a facility, enter an ✓, x, N/A, or complete the space with other appropriate response.

[✓ - Document required for facility category is complete and current.
x - Document is lacking, incomplete or requires updating
N/A - Not applicable]

Any item shown as "x" shall be documented on the Licensing Report (LIC 809) with a plan of correction date. File this form in the facility file.

FACILITY NAME	LICENSE REPORT (LIC 809) DATE
FACILITY NUMBER	TYPE OF VISIT ☐ PRELICENSING ☐ RENEWAL ☐ EVALUATION ☐ COMPLAINT ☐ FOLLOW-UP

*REFERENCE NUMBER	NAME OF CLIENT/RESIDENT	ENTER DATE OF BIRTH	ADMISSION AGREEMENT	ENTER DATE OF ADMISSION	SOURCE OF INCOME	IDENTIFICATION AND EMERGENCY INFO	MEDICAL ASSESSMENT	AMBULATORY STATUS	T.B. TEST	CONSENT FORMS	APPRAISAL AND NEEDS AND SERVICES PLAN	SAFEGUARDS FOR CASH RESOURCES	ENTER INFO REGARDING CASH RESOURCES FROM EACH LEDGER	SAFEGUARDS FOR PROPERTY/VALUABLES	PERSONAL RIGHTS	WEIGHT RECORD	IMMUNIZATION RECORD	CENTRALLY STORED DESTROYED MEDICATION RECORDS	ENTER DATE OF DISCHARGE	COMMENTS
													BAL. / DATE							
													BAL. / DATE							
													BAL. / DATE							
													BAL. / DATE							
													BAL. / DATE							
													BAL. / DATE							
													BAL. / DATE							
													BAL. / DATE							
													BAL. / DATE							
													BAL. / DATE							
													BAL. / DATE							
													BAL. / DATE							
													BAL. / DATE							
													BAL. / DATE							
													BAL. / DATE							

LICENSING EVALUATOR SIGNATURE	DATE

*Reference number corresponds to number used to identify individual client/resident on the field visit report.

LIC 858 (10/99)CONFIDENTIAL

STATE OF CALIFORNIA - HEALTH AND HUMAN SERVICES AGENCY

CALIFORNIA DEPARTMENT OF SOCIAL SERVICES

AGENCY - FOSTER PARENTS AGREEMENT

Child Placed by Agency in Foster Home

Complete in Duplicate:
One copy to: Foster parents
Child's Social Service Record

The agreement will be initiated when the child is placed in the facility and whenever the rate changes.

NAME OF CHILD		PARENT'S NAME
BIRTHDATE OF CHILD	DATE PLACED	CASE NUMBER
FOSTER PARENT'S NAME		ADDRESS

Anticipated duration of placement is ________ months.

The agency will pay $ __________ per __________ for room and board, clothing, personal needs, recreation, transportation, education, incidentals and supervision. First payment to be within 45 days after placement with subsequent payments no later than the 15th of the month following provision of care.

If additional amounts are to be paid, the reason, amount and conditions shall be set forth here:. ______________________________

____

Special problems/needs: ☐ No ☐ Yes If yes, explain. ______________________________

Special Permissions: Special permission for substitute supervision is subject to Community Care Licensing granting an exception to the licensing regulation, which requires that substitute supervision in the foster home be limited to an adult.

☐ Child 15 years or older has permission to remain without adult supervision during temporary absences of the the foster parent(s), not to exceed six (6) consecutive hours in any one 72-hour period.

☐ Substitute supervision may be provided to the foster child by someone 16 years of age or older (not a foster child) during temporary absences of the foster parent(s), not to exceed six (6) consecutive hours in any one 72-hour period.

☐ Other (Explain) ______________________________

☐ No special permissions granted.

AGENCY AGREES TO

1. Provide the foster parent with educational stability requirement, school of origin and travel plan, knowledge of the background and needs of the child necessary for effective care. This may include a social work assessment, medical reports, education assessment, and identification of special needs when necessary. This shall be made available to foster parents within 14 days from date of placement.
2. Develop a plan for the child and share pertinent aspects with the foster parents.
3. Inform foster parents they may give the same consents on behalf of the child as the parent, except for those prohibitions provided in Social Services Manual Regulations.
4. Not remove the child with less than 7 calendar days written notice unless: the child is physically or psychologically endangered; court orders removal; parents or guardians order removal (voluntary placement); signed waiver obtained from foster parents; removal is from an interim placement directly into an adoptive home.
5. Involve foster parents in future planning for the child. The placement shall be reviewed within 6 months.
6. Assist the child in his use of foster care.
7. Assist in the maintenance of the child's constructive relationships with parents and other family members and to involve parents in future planning for this child.
8. Provide procedure for grievances of foster parents.
9. Contact the child and foster parents at least once a month. If case plan would indicate less frequent contacts, the foster parent will be informed.
10. Inform foster parents if child has any tendencies toward dangerous behavior.
11. Provide Medi-Cal card or other medical coverage at time of placement. Arrange for medical examination within 30 days unless child has had such within past 6 months and information is available.
12. Provide a clothing allowance as permitted to meet initial clothing needs.
13. In cooperation with foster parents arrange for visiting by parents or relatives on: ______________________________.
14. Provide arrangements for school of origin travel as appropriate.
15. Provide assistance with emergencies. Telephone number for after-hours or weekends is: ______________________________.

***See Next Page for Optional Long-Term Placement Intent**

FOSTER PARENTS AGREE TO

1. Provide this child the nurture, care, clothing and training suited to his needs.
2. Develop an understanding of the responsibilities, objectives, and requirements of the Agency in regard to the care of this child.
3. Recognize the Agency's responsibility for planning for this child, as given by the court or the parent(s).
4. Recognize any limitations of consent imposed by the court or the parent.
5. Increase their knowledge and ability to care for this child.
6. Encourage the child's relationships with his parents and relatives.
7. Cooperate in visiting arrangements between child and parents.
8. Not use corporal punishment, punishment in the presence of others, deprivation of meals, monetary allowances, visit from parent, home visits, threat of removal or any type of degrading or humiliating punishment, and to use constructive alternative methods of discipline.
9. Respect and keep confidential information given about the child and his family.
10. Immediately notify agency of significant changes in this child's health, behavior, or location.
11. Accept the child's special problems as given above in my provision of care.
12. Help with termination of placement including return to his own parents, relatives home, or adoptive placement.
13. Give the agency prior notice of at least 7 days if removal of child is requested unless it is agreed upon with the agency that less time is necessary.
14. Conform to the licensing/certification requirements.
15. Provide state and federal agencies access to documentation when documentation is maintained on children in their care.
16. Give advance written notice to the licensing agency and the person or agency responsible for the child of any (foster parent(s)) absence of 48 hours or longer. (Absence may be reported by telephone in case of emergencies.)
17. Notify the agency immediately if an application is made on behalf of this child for any kind of income. Examples of income include, but are not limited to, child support payments, Veterans Benefits, Railroad Retirement, Social Security, RSHDI, and Supplemental Security Income/State Supplemental Program (SSI/SSP).
18. Remit to Department of Public Social Services any income received on behalf of this child while in foster care up to the full cost of board and care plus medical cost. In addition, I will cooperate to have the Social Security Administration, or the appropriate agency, make the Department of Public Social Services the payee for any funds received on behalf of this child.
19. Foster parent agrees to immediately notify the placing agency of any changes to the child's educational travel, withdrawal from school or graduation.

SOC 156 (12/11) REQUIRED FORM - NO SUBSTITUTE PERMITTED

PAGE 1 OF 2

Print

SUSPECTED CHILD ABUSE REPORT

Reset Form

To Be Completed by **Mandated Child Abuse Reporters**
Pursuant to Penal Code Section 11166

PLEASE PRINT OR TYPE

CASE NAME: ______________________

CASE NUMBER: ______________________

A. REPORTING PARTY

NAME OF MANDATED REPORTER	TITLE	MANDATED REPORTER CATEGORY
REPORTER'S BUSINESS/AGENCY NAME AND ADDRESS Street City Zip		DID MANDATED REPORTER WITNESS THE INCIDENT? ☐ YES ☐ NO
REPORTER'S TELEPHONE (DAYTIME) ( )	SIGNATURE	TODAY'S DATE

B. REPORT NOTIFICATION

☐ LAW ENFORCEMENT ☐ COUNTY PROBATION ☐ COUNTY WELFARE / CPS (Child Protective Services)	AGENCY
ADDRESS Street City Zip	DATE/TIME OF PHONE CALL
OFFICIAL CONTACTED - TITLE	TELEPHONE ( )

C. VICTIM One report per victim

NAME (LAST, FIRST, MIDDLE)	BIRTHDATE OR APPROX. AGE	SEX	ETHNICITY
ADDRESS Street City Zip	TELEPHONE ( )		
PRESENT LOCATION OF VICTIM	SCHOOL	CLASS	GRADE
PHYSICALLY DISABLED? ☐ YES ☐ NO	DEVELOPMENTALLY DISABLED? ☐ YES ☐ NO	OTHER DISABILITY (SPECIFY)	PRIMARY LANGUAGE SPOKEN IN HOME
IN FOSTER CARE? ☐ YES ☐ NO	IF VICTIM WAS IN OUT-OF-HOME CARE AT TIME OF INCIDENT, CHECK TYPE OF CARE: ☐ DAY CARE ☐ CHILD CARE CENTER ☐ FOSTER FAMILY HOME ☐ FAMILY FRIEND ☐ GROUP HOME OR INSTITUTION ☐ RELATIVE'S HOME		TYPE OF ABUSE (CHECK ONE OR MORE) ☐ PHYSICAL ☐ MENTAL ☐ SEXUAL ☐ NEGLECT ☐ OTHER (SPECIFY)
RELATIONSHIP TO SUSPECT	PHOTOS TAKEN? ☐ YES ☐ NO		DID THE INCIDENT RESULT IN THIS VICTIM'S DEATH? ☐ YES ☐ NO ☐ UNK

D. INVOLVED PARTIES

VICTIM'S SIBLINGS

	NAME	BIRTHDATE	SEX	ETHNICITY		NAME	BIRTHDATE	SEX	ETHNICITY
1					3				
2					4				

VICTIM'S PARENTS/GUARDIANS

NAME (LAST, FIRST, MIDDLE)		BIRTHDATE OR APPROX. AGE	SEX	ETHNICITY
ADDRESS Street City Zip	HOME PHONE ( )	BUSINESS PHONE ( )		
NAME (LAST, FIRST, MIDDLE)		BIRTHDATE OR APPROX. AGE	SEX	ETHNICITY
ADDRESS Street City Zip	HOME PHONE ( )	BUSINESS PHONE ( )		

SUSPECT

SUSPECT'S NAME (LAST, FIRST, MIDDLE)	BIRTHDATE OR APPROX. AGE	SEX	ETHNICITY
ADDRESS Street City Zip	TELEPHONE ( )		
OTHER RELEVANT INFORMATION			

E. INCIDENT INFORMATION

IF NECESSARY, ATTACH EXTRA SHEET(S) OR OTHER FORM(S) AND CHECK THIS BOX ☐ *IF MULTIPLE VICTIMS, INDICATE NUMBER* ______

DATE / TIME OF INCIDENT	PLACE OF INCIDENT
NARRATIVE DESCRIPTION (What victim(s) said/what the mandated reporter observed/what person accompanying the victim(s) said/similar or past incidents involving the victim(s) or suspect)	

SS 8572 (Rev. 12/02)

DEFINITIONS AND INSTRUCTIONS ON REVERSE

DO NOT submit a copy of this form to the Department of Justice (DOJ). The investigating agency is required under Penal Code Section 11169 to submit to DOJ a Child Abuse Investigation Report Form SS 8583 if (1) an active investigation was conducted and (2) the incident was determined not to be unfounded.

WHITE COPY-Police or Sheriff's Department; BLUE COPY-County Welfare or Probation Department; GREEN COPY- District Attorney's Office; YELLOW COPY-Reporting Party

JV-220 Application Regarding Psychotropic Medication

Clerk stamps date here when form is filed.

To keep other people from seeing what you entered on your form, please press the Clear This Form button at the end of the form when finished.

Attach a completed and signed JV-220(A), *Prescribing Physician's Statement—Attachment,* with all its attachments, must be attached to this form before it is filed with the court. Read JV-219-INFO, *Information About Psychotropic Medication Forms,* for more information about the required forms and the application process.

Fill in court name and street address:

Superior Court of California, County of

Fill in child's name and date of birth:

Child's Name:

Date of Birth:

Clerk fills in case number when form is filed.

Case Number:

(1) Information about where the child lives:

a. The child lives ☐ with a relative ☐ in a foster home
☐ with a nonrelative extended family member
☐ in a regular group home ☐ in a level 12–14 group home
☐ at a juvenile camp ☐ at a juvenile ranch
☐ other *(specify)*: ______________________

b. If applicable, name of facility where child lives: ______________________

c. Contact information for responsible adult where child lives:
(1) Name: ______________________
(2) Phone: ______________________

(2) Information about the child's current location:

a. ☐ The child remains at the location identified in (1).
b. ☐ The child is currently staying in:
(1) ☐ a psychiatric hospital *(name)*: ______________________
(2) ☐ a juvenile hall *(name)*: ______________________
(3) ☐ other *(specify)*: ______________________

(3) Child's ☐ social worker ☐ probation officer

a. Name: ______________________
b. Address: ______________________
c. Phone: ______________ Fax: ______________

(4) Number of pages attached: ______

Date: ______________

______________________ ▶ ______________________
Type or print name of person completing this form *Signature*

☐ Child welfare services staff *(sign above)*
☐ Probation department staff *(sign above)*
☐ Medical office staff *(sign above)*
☐ Caregiver *(sign above)*
☐ Prescribing physician *(sign on page 3 of JV-220(A))*

Judicial Council of California, www.courtinfo.ca.gov
Revised January 1, 2008, Mandatory Form
Welfare and Institutions Code, § 369.5
California Rules of Court, rule 5.640

Application Regarding Psychotropic Medication

JV-220, Page 1 of 1

www.ingramcontent.com/pod-product-compliance
Lightning Source LLC
Chambersburg PA
CBHW030432290526
45786CB00001B/249